D0564302

Coyote Cowboy Poetry

By Baxter Black

illustrated by Don Gill and Bob Black

with help from

Jay Adams
Jan Swan Gifford
Cheryl Hawes
Charles Marsh
Ace Reid
Sue Rosoff
Theresa Schleigh

COYOTE COWBOY COMPANY

Benson 1986

All poems written by Baxter Black

Published by: Coyote Cowboy Company
P.O. Box 2190
Benson, Arizona 85602

Cover design by Jay Dusard

LIBRARY OF CONGRESS CATALOGING IN PUBLICATION DATA

Main entry under:
Cowboy Poetry

Bibliography: p
1. Coyote Cowboy Poetry
2. Cowboys-Poetry
3. Poetry-Cowboy
4. Humor-Cowboy
5. Agriculture-Poetic Comment

I. Black, Baxter, 1945-

Library of Congress #86-061745
ISBN 0-939343-00-2

OTHER BOOKS BY BAXTER

* THE COWBOY AND HIS DOG © 1980
* A RIDER, A ROPER AND A HECK'UVA WINDMILL MAN © 1982
ON THE EDGE OF COMMON SENSE, THE BEST SO FAR © 1983
* DOC, WHILE YER HERE © 1984
BUCKAROO HISTORY © 1985
✓ CROUTONS ON A COW PIE © 1988
✓ THE BUCKSKIN MARE © 1989
✓ COWBOY STANDARD TIME © 1990
CROUTONS ON A COW PIE, VOL 2 © 1992
HEY, COWBOY, WANNA GET LUCKY? © 1994 *(Crown Publishing, Inc)*
DUNNY AND THE DUCK © 1994

** included in their entirety in Coyote Cowboy Poetry © 1986*
✓ included in their entirety in Croutons On A Cow Pie, Vol 2 © 1992

FOREWORD

It is easy and a temptation to compare Baxter Black's wit and humor to Will Rogers; his poetry and songs to Curley Fletcher, Bruce Kiskaddon, S. Omar Barker, and even to Robert Frost; and his radio and newspaper commentaries to major network/newspaper personalities; but to do so is unfair to Baxter. Each of the aforementioned is a person who developed his own style of writing and presentation and attracted a following and emulators. Baxter has developed his own style of writing and presentation and has attracted his own admirers and emulators. Thus, he doesn't need to be compared to others; he can stand with pride along side Will Rogers, Curley Fletcher and other great creative, talented Westerners.

This collection of poetry contains "something old and something new"; it does not contain anything "borrowed" or "blue." It contains his reflections, observations, and thoughts about life in the West in the 20th Century — commentaries in verse that make us laugh at our everyday problems and attitudes. However, emotions other than humor are expressed. Baxter has chosen to ride the least ridden trail — that of the humorist who makes a person laugh at himself, not others.

I was with Baxter one cold snowy December evening in Cody, Wyoming, and saw ranching families who had driven over one hundred miles just to meet him; no honor can be so great and no words can compare to that testimony, when his peers show such admiration and affection.

Through the years in his other books, many companions have ridden with him and provided illustrations; two have been steady companions — his long time friend Don Gill and his brother Bob Black. Their illustrations and cartoons visualize his words with the perfection of wit and humor that come only from mutual respect and love.

Baxter's previous books sold over 50,000 copies. He gives over 100 programs a year. His weekly column, which often features his poetry, is widely syndicated. It is safe to say that Baxter is one of the most widely read and heard poets in this nation. Hopefully, with the renewed interest in cowboy poetry and with this new, enlarged collection, Baxter will receive and enjoy an even broader audience and appreciation — he has earned it.

Dr. Guy Logsdon
Professor of Education and American Folklife
University of Tulsa

Guy Logsdon is a folklorist by interest and has collected cowboy lore, songs and poetry for many years and has written many articles about the songs.

TABLE OF CONTENTS

TABLE OF CONTENTS (continued)

With special thanks to
Sheryl Suhr, friend and secretary,
Harry Green and Dan Green
and the Record Stockman Staff . . .

. . . and dedicated to Cindy Lou

"Ambition feeds a thousand fires
Whose ashes leave no ember.
I pray to pen a rustic rhyme
That someone will remember."

Carlos Ashley

The Spur

I came to a low water crossing
Where the trails converged near the bank
And all by itself, I spotted a spur
That lay buried plum up to the shank.

I kicked at the dirt all around it
But its mate was not to be found
Then I wondered just what circumstances
Had led to this spur in the ground.

This trail, no doubt, had been traveled
By sinner and saint in the past
And the spur was a quiet reminder
That leather and muscle don't last.

It might have belonged to a bandit
Who was hanged by the neck from a tree,
A settler who drowned on his way to the west;
A drifter who longed to breathe free.

It might have belonged to a cowpoke
Who bucked off a renegade bronc
Or lost by two lovers one romantic night
On the way back from some honky tonk.

A trapper, a scout, a brave buckaroo,
A panner who died for his claim,
The spur stood alone, an unexplained story,
A headstone awaiting a name.

I finally unraveled the mystery
My answer was there in the sands.
The tracks of his horse went round in a circle,
The spur was a one leg-ged man's.

GARCIA
J.M. CAPRIOLA
ELKO, NEV.
BOB BLACK

COYOTE COWBOY PROVERBS

- Breakfast is the most important meal of the day. If you ain't home by then, boy, yer in real trouble.
- You can lead a horse to water, but you can't make a silk purse out of him.
- It is impossible to insult a rude person.
- Wherever two or more are gathered in the name of animal rights, there shall the press be also.
- The public will support agriculture 'til the last tractor is repossessed or the price of food goes up, whichever comes first.
- Dogs and old men thrive on monotony.
- I'm so miserable without you, it's like you never left.
- We eat pretty good when da company comes.
- A hundred pounds of salt is heavier than a hundred pounds of anything else.
- Windier than a sack full of whistlin' lips.
- A first class manager hires first class help. A second class manager hires third class help.
- When given a choice, a cow will always go out the wrong gate.

COYOTE COWBOY PROVERBS

- Always wear a tie the color of the main course.
- Nobody loves a wet dog.
- Free advice is always worth more than advice you have to pay for.
- Tequila never lets you forget, but it doesn't care what you do.
- A bird in the hand beats two pair.
- The eyelids of the bureaucracy are upon you.
- Good public servants vote for what's in their heart. Good politicians vote for what's in their hand.
- Profits, like prayers, often get put on hold.
- The secret to good management is good help and enough of it.
- Two's a coincidence, three's an epidemic.
- A cowboy should have three things: a good dog, a good horse, and an inflatable rubber woman.
- The lawyer's motto: an eye for an eyelash.
- The large print giveth and the small print taketh away.
- Smart as a busload of county agents.
- Timing has a lot to do with the success of a rain dance.

THE COWBOY AND THE LADY

She was tall and seductive, limber and lean
Right off she caught his eye.
She marched with a purpose right up to the door
That he was standin' by

He took off his hat and reached for the knob
And started to open the door
She spun on her heels and glared in his face
And under her breath she swore.

She said, "The last thing I need is a cowboy
Who thinks I'm a frail fraulein
And tries to impress me with sweet talk
With candlelight, roses and wine!"

"All men are alike, I've decided.
You're only after one thing!
All your chivalrous ways don't mean doodly!
There's no way I'm gonna swing!"

Then she made him an obscene gesture
And stepped back to give him the space.
But he let the door slip from his fingers
And it hit'er right square in the face!

'Cause his mother had gave him instructions
'Bout women, and others advise:
To treat each one like a lady,
Until she can prove otherwise!

TUCOMCARY
MERC
SINCE 300 BC
DRINK SLUDGE
CLOSED
Don ... 1980 ©

VANISHING BREED?

They call'em a vanishing breed.
They write books and take pictures
    and talk like they're all dyin' out.
Like dinosaurs goin' to seed
But that's my friends yer talkin' about.

Like Tex from Juniper Mountain.
He carved out a way of life
    where only the toughest prevail.
He's fifty-seven an' countin'.
His sons now follow his trail.

And Mike who still ain't got married.
At home in the seat of a saddle,
    a sagebrush aristocrat.
I reckon that's how he'll be buried;
A'horseback, still wearin' his hat.

There's Bryan, Albert and Floyd.
Cowmen as good as the legends
    to whom their livelihood's linked,
Who'd be just a little annoyed
To know they're considered extinct.

Some say they're endangered species
Destined to fade into footnotes
    like ropes that never get throwed.
To that I reply, "Bull Feces!"
They're just hard to see from the road.

QUARTER CIRCLE W, N.M. / RAIN BARREL, AZ / CRESENT F, CA. / FLYING U, NE / SAFETY PIN, N.M / OK, TX / BAR FORTY, TX
WHANGDOODLE, N.M / DOUBLE A, TX / HALF DIAMOND H, N.M. / CIRCLE STAR, CA / TWO BIT, AZ / ROCKING R, TX
HEART FOUR BAR, TX / TEJON, CA / HATCHET, NM / CIRCLE A BAR, CA.

THE OLD DAYS

The little kid sat on his knee
And looked up with stars in his eyes
He said, Grandaddy, tell me again
How it was when you were my size

The old man remembered with care
And the memories flooded his mind
He said it was wild and free in the west
But that was before your time.

I had me a little blue roan
And son, he could run like the wind
And right over there where the parking lot is
We raced and always would win.

Where they put up the State Valley Bank
The Indians would camp on the site
And the very first antelope herd that I saw
Was right at the new signal light

And down by the furniture store
Where every week they have a sale
The Overland Stage at the end of each week
Would come by and drop off the mail.

And, oh, I remember the time
When Buffalo Bill all alone
Caught up with the Daltons and they shot it out
It was down by the savings and loan.

And Grandma, may she rest in peace,
Would wait for me down by the strand
And finally, one day, I gave her a ring.
That spot's now a hamburger stand.

Asphalt and pavement now run
Over all of my boyhood days
People need people and out west they came
But I don't begrudge'm their ways.

Oh, yes, it was different back then
And everything's changed so it seems
But deep in my heart I miss it sometimes
So I have to go back in my dreams.

THE MECHANICAL COWBOY

A ringy ol' cow can make me so mad
My skin gets hot to the touch
But I git a heap madder, I'll tellya,
When I have a slippin' clutch.

There's somethin' about mechanical things
That's worse than a naggin' wife.
They acquire some kind of annoyin' twitch
And then seem to come to life.

The dadgum release on handyman jacks,
A bolt that never quite fits;
Phillips screwdrivers with heads wore plum out
Give me the shiverin' fits.

A comf'terbul cab that leaks like a sieve,
Sprockets that won't hold a chain,
And tryin' to change a tire in your suit
Goin' to church in the rain.

Now, I'd lots rather put in a prolapse
Or handle a bitin' dog
As work on a baler that ain't tyin' right
Or augers that just won't aug.

Or them motors that's all time a'dyin',
Sprayers that drizzle and drip,
Electrical breakers that sizzle and crack
And clippers that druther not clip.

I'm plum sick and tired of fightin' them things
Made outta plastic and steel.
There's days I believe, I'd strangle that man,
The one that invented the wheel.

As you might have guessed by hearin' me talk
For sure, I'm no fixit man.
There ain't no walkin' disaster that's worse than
Me with a wrench in my hand.

I could trade places with Adam of Olde
And still never get relief.
My wife, good ol' Eve, would need somethin' fixed;
She'd probably have a loose leaf!

WHO'D A THOUGHT THAT HELD THAT SUCKER TOGETHER
© 1982

LOUIE AND THE TONGS

Let me tell ya 'bout Louie.

We's workin' a bunch of replacement heifers a couple years ago up on the Little Willow. Louie runs the cows. It was kind of a hot day an' we's workin' those critters through the chute.

Clyde and Monte wuz there an' they wuz pushin'em in. I wuz runnin' the squeeze on the ol' Teco chute and Louie wuz runnin' the head.

What Louie'd do is reach around an' grab the heifer as she come in, snap the nose tongs on'er nose and pull'er up snug. Then I'd come around an' draw a little blood outta the jugular for the Bangs test so we could get'em cleared by the government.

It wuz August, hot, 'bout ninety degrees. You know when you're workin' them cows an' it's hot like that it ain't very comfortable. The way he'd do it, we'd run the heifer in and catch'er. Then Louie'd reach down and bend over and pick up those tongs and slap'em on. Then when we's done with her he'd jus' throw them tongs back on the ground an' let'er out.

'Bout the middle of the second day it dawned on him that it wuz shore tiresome work bendin' over, pickin' up them tongs every time so he tied the shank of the nose tongs onto his belt. Tied'em good, ya know. Then all he had to do when one come in wuz jus' grab that shank, flip'er up and catch them tongs and snap'em on, dally and drag'er up. Then when he was done he'd jus' drop'em an' he didn't have to bend over and pick'em up every time.

Oh, he was proud! We got to braggin' on him, callin' him the Tong Champion and such. He got to flippin' it behind his back, through his legs and around his head. Kinda broke up the monotony of the day.

Then one of these heifers come a roarin' in, boy, jus' like a freight train! She stuck both her front feet through that Teco, ya know, like they can do in those chutes. Louie got her mashed down good and I had her hip-locked with the squeeze. We didn't want to let her go 'cause we'd had to go get her outta the bunch we'd already done and so, anyway, it wuz worth it to hold onto her. So I wuz mashin' her fer all I was worth and I hollered to Lou to get a hold of her head. Then I jumped over on the head bar and set on it real good while Louie run up and grabbed her.

Now, Louie's a big fella, well over six foot and stout an' strong; a big swede. He jus' stepped up, grabbed her around the neck like a bulldogger and held her there. He reached down with his left hand and snapped them tongs on her snout. He was holdin' her there and I'll be damned if she didn't git out!

Off we went! Just as she escaped I got her by the tail with both hands and in two jumps she was goin' flat out! I wuz sailin' behind her like a water skiier! Louie wuz runnin' neck an' neck with her 'round that corral tryin' to keep slack in the line so he could get that knot untied and keep from gettin' drug to death!

He wuddn't havin' any luck.

Tryin' to keep his eye peeled for the railroad ties and old posts layin' around the corral and she never even slowed down when she hit the trash barrel and set junk to flyin' everywhere!

Louie wuz runnin' right beside her, boy, takin' great big steps, his eyes were 'bout that big around and he kept screamin', "Don't let'er go, boys, don't let'er go!"

She made a complete pass around that corral and come to a stop in the corner right in front of the chute. We's all settin' there heavin' and breathin' like a Kenworth and Louie wuz madly tryin' to get that knot untied and I wuz jus' doubled over with laughter!

The corner consisted of the corral fence and an eight foot Powder River gate that went into the next pen.

Out of the side of my vision, through my teary eyes, I seen a hand reach out and flip that bar on the Powder River gate and that gate swung open real easy. The heifer spied the opening and shot through that hole like a rocket!

Boy! Straight out into the big corral makin' a bee-line for the pasture gate and about half way across'er I jus' couldn't tak'er any more and crashed to the ground. The dust is boilin' up and the last thing I see 'fore I go down is Louie out on the end of that tong rope, swingin' like a rock in David's slingshot!

When the dust settled he was layin' there up against the fence in a crumpled heap, fingering the broken end of the rope like the beads on his rosary.

THE COWBOY'S GOIN' HOLLYWOOD

I was settin' in a cafe eatin' chili dogs and fries
When I spied an ol' cowpuncher I knew from days gone by.
I didn't recognize him 'cause he'd let his hair grow long.
He came and sat beside me but somethin' else was wrong.

He wore a brand new Stetson that didn't have a mark
With a silver concho hat band made of twisted quakie bark.
Once he'd worn a felt one, old and black as sin,
That he used to feed his pony and change the oil in.

His shirts were always dirty, the worst I'd ever known,
But the one that he was wearin' looked like an ice cream cone.
He had a turquoise watch band, was chewin' juju beans
And traded his ol' levi's for starched designer jeans.

He wore a silver buckle, the kind you'd never win,
His Justin resoled cowhides were now iguana skin.
His old five buckle sloggers, he'd kept held up with twine,
He'd replaced with little rubbers, so dainty and refined.

He now drank gin and tonic, drove a Cadillac around
And lived in an apartment in the center of a town.
He said he'd been discovered by a Nashville record man
And traveled o'er the country with a bus and five piece band.

I felt a little sorry fer my ol' cowpunchin' pard
But the more I thought about it, it couldn't be that hard.
I think my ol' friend needs me to help him count his blessin's
So first thing Monday mornin', I start my singin' lessons.

HEY, I'M RAY
BILLY BEER
MENU
BOB BLACK

THE COWBOY POETRY GATHERING

I went to the first annual ever
convention of cowboy bards.
(I woulda said poets, but poet's a word
that sure makes a rhymer's job hard)
There were buckaroos, pokes and vaqueros,
poppers and drovers and jakes,
Mule ridin' packers, some crazy colt sackers,
and even a couple of snakes.

They converged on the small town of Elko
that's seen more than one rubber check
But this many poets all stumblin' around
was worse than a railroad wreck.
They had come from the ranches and cowtowns,
their poetry burstin' their brains
And any poor fool on a corner or stool
was subjected to endless refrains.

There were poems about dyin' a'horseback.
Poems about shootin' a bear.
There even were poems about ol' beat up cowpokes
bemoanin' the loss of their hair.
Of course, there were poems about horses
and punchers in town gettin' fleeced,
And poems about dogs, though none about hogs,
which I don't regret in the least.

But with so many cowboy poets
and so many stories to tell,
Not every poem that we'd ever written
got read, though we tried, to beat hell.
Part of the problem I reckon, was time,
and therein, good friends, was the pinch
'Cause each planned to disclose a mile of prose
and was asked to recite just an inch!

NUAL
OWBO
ET
PAYROLL
BOB BLACK

THE NEW HAT

Yesterday I went to buy myself a brand new hat
'Cause the one I had was bent all outta shape.
The brim was gettin' soggy and the crown was beat to hell
And I'd patched the holes inside with bits o' tape.

So, I asked the lady waitin' and she pointed to the wall.
Them hats were lined up like a marchin' band!
I thought she was mistaken so I asked her once again,
"M'am, I want a new one, not a second hand."

'Cause them hats all looked like victims of the second world war!
Reminders of the times when I was broke.
When I had to wear my Stetson 'til my head showed through the top.
But then, I figgered, maybe it's a joke?

But that lady never smiled as she held one up with pride.
She remarked that it would surely suit me fine!
Why, it was doubled over like a shovel bent in two
And the sweat band was already grease and grime!

It had a little copy of a can o' Lone Star beer
And an extra you could pin upon yer shirt
With a shiny silver emblem clingin' boldly to the band
That said, "Bulldoggers do it in the dirt!"

It was covered up with feathers like a peacock in the moult
I'm here to tellya it was quite a sight!
I lacked the heart to tell'er, I couldn't wear a hat
That looked just like two chickens in a fight!

So I took my old Resistol and I stuck it on my head
And made my way out through the swingin' doors
When a feller spied me leavin' and said, "This must be the place!
I come to git a cowboy hat like yours!"

That day I learned a lesson and sold that kid my hat
Now I've gathered up my laundry in a box
And I'm down in front of Shepler's sellin' antique western wear,
You wanna buy a pair of cowboy socks?

THE MERC
SALE TODAY
25% OFF
AUTHENTIC COWBOY CLOTHES For SALE
OPEN
1982 ©

OCCUPATION: COWBOY

WANTED: Cowboy. No TV, no phone. If you don't like dogs and can't tough it in the mountains, don't apply.

Alamo, Nevada

Somebody said, "YOU A COWBOY?"
I said, "I reckon it's so."
"WELL, WHERE'S ALL YER GUNS AND YER FEATHERY HAT!
AND HOW COME YER SADDLE'S SO OLD?"

"I SEEN A COWBOY IN NASHVILLE!
HE SURE LOOKED TO ME TO BE LIVE.
HIS HAT WAS BEAT UP BUT THE FEATHERS WUZ NEW
AND HIS PICKUP WAS FOUR WHEEL DRIVE!"

"HIS BOOTS WAS SILVER AND TURQUOISE.
HIS BUCKLE SAID *DRINK LONE STAR BEER!*
I ASKED IF HE'D RODE THE MECHANICAL BULL.
'OF COURSE' he said, 'WITHOUT FEAR.' "

I stopped this inquirin' stranger
And to ignorance chalked up his talk.
He didn't have no more idea in hell
Whether cows could fly or could walk.

I said, "Mister, if you want to find out
Who's cowboy and who's playin' games,
Read OCCUPATION on my IRS form.
Sometimes a man ain't all he claims!"

THE PARADOX

The saddle on the rack was priced at thirteen hundred bucks
Handmade and stamped with flowers to impress the mucky mucks.
An A fork tree and double rigged, but what you noticed most;
The dally horn rose from the swells just like a cedar post.

The rawhide reins and latigo were first class all the way
'Cause quality in leather goods might save yer life someday.
The custom made-to-order boots with seventeen inch tops
Would keep you safe from rattlesnakes; three hundred bucks a pop!

Scarves of raw imported silk in reds and blues and greens.
And Wranglers, cause no western man would wear generic jeans.
Designer shirts with monograms embroidered on the cuff
And silver Copenhagen cans to hold a gourmet's snuff.

A hundred dollar ten X hat and leggin's made to fit
Inlaid spurs and slobber chains to match the silver bit
There's everything a man could want to ride the range in style
Yet there's a paradox exists, that doesn't reconcile.

It's ironic in this day and age of Xerox cowboy folks
That real, git up everyday and ride fer pay, cowpokes
Can see the best authentic tack presented on display
But can't afford to buy it on a cowboy's meager pay!

Buckaroo Specials
Saddle -$2500.00
CHINKS $275.00
REATA -$100.00
HATS From $185.00
86

THE COWBOY AND HIS TAPEWORM

The world is on a diet. Seems, no matter where you look
Every fruitcake with a recipe has got a diet book.
But I think if they were honest, I'll bet they'd all concede
The omniverous indifference of a cowboy's all you need.

He's in tune with Mother Nature and can live off of the land
From the mountains of Montana to the muddy Rio Grande.
He's the ultimate consumer, he'll eat anything he finds.
I've seen'em lick the peelin' paint off Forest Service signs.

Or chew a steel fence post just to get down to the meat.
He'll eat playin' cards and bob wire; anything a cow would eat.
A drumstick from a buzzard, a wilted Christmas wreath
Then finish with a porcupine just to pick his teeth.

He'll drink water from a cow track, eat the claws of grizzly bear
And you won't find no leftovers, he eats feathers, bone and hair.
He makes hunters run for cover, he scares hikers half to death
And he leaves no trace behind him, just the smell of his bad breath.

If you doubt what I have told you, I assure you that it's right,
I have painted you a picture of a cowboy's appetite.
Though it may not look too pretty, it's exactly like I've drawn it.
He'd prob'ly eat a bale of hay if you put whiskey on it.

So the world keeps on a'joggin' and a'sippin' diet pop
But the cowboy and his tapeworm ride the range and eat non-stop.
If yer overweight and worried, you should dine with him a while,
'Cause there ain't no chubby cowboys in existence, in the wild.

BURP!

THE ROOSTER WITH SPURS

Down at the Smith Barn one day we wuz calvin' first calf heifers. Now a lot of the boys that don't speak English real good have to make up their own names for the gringos. They have trouble sayin' them English names like Carruthers or Mackintosh and the like. They sound common to us but they ain't common to them. Their name fer Dale, just to give you an idea of what kinda guy he is, is "Gallo con espuellas" which is "the Rooster with Spurs." He does kinda walk with his chest out, sorta cocky and wears them big ol' jinglin' rowels. Always wears a bright scarf.

He come a stridin' in down there one mornin' pretty early just dressed up fit to kill. Brand new shirt and everything! Really proud! George had been there all night and he had a heifer in the squeeze chute tryin' to pull this calf. He'd pulled fer all he's worth and wuz plum give out. Dale saw him and said, "Whattsa matter? Can't you pull that calf? Git outta the way and let me do it!"

George wuddn't 'bout to argue. He'd been workin' on him fer a while anyway.

Dale stepped around there behind the heifer, propped his feet up against the bottom of the chute, grabbed a holt of them two OB handles and jis' rared back!

The calf wuz comin' straight out and had his head jus' right, he's a big calf wuz all. Dale, whenever he gits to doin' somethin' he grits his teeth and smiles jus' like a jack-o-lantern and squints his eyes. He had a good grip and wuz leaned back like a water skiier.

As the calf started to come, that nice smooth little round forehead on the calf pressed up on the heifer's rectum and cleaned it slicker'n a whistle! There was a stream 'bout an eighth of an inch thick and two inches wide came arcin' out like a rainbow. It jus' missed the brim of Dale's hat an' splattered all over his face, in his mouth and down the front of his shirt. He couldn't do nothin' cause he was rared back so far. If he'da let go he'da fell flat on his back! So he jus' hung on 'til the calf came out and crashed in a soggy pile on top of him!

We went over and dragged the calf offa him. Dale come to life spittin' and cussin'! He raised his head just in time to see that heifer, pretty as ya please, clean the afterbirth right in his lap!

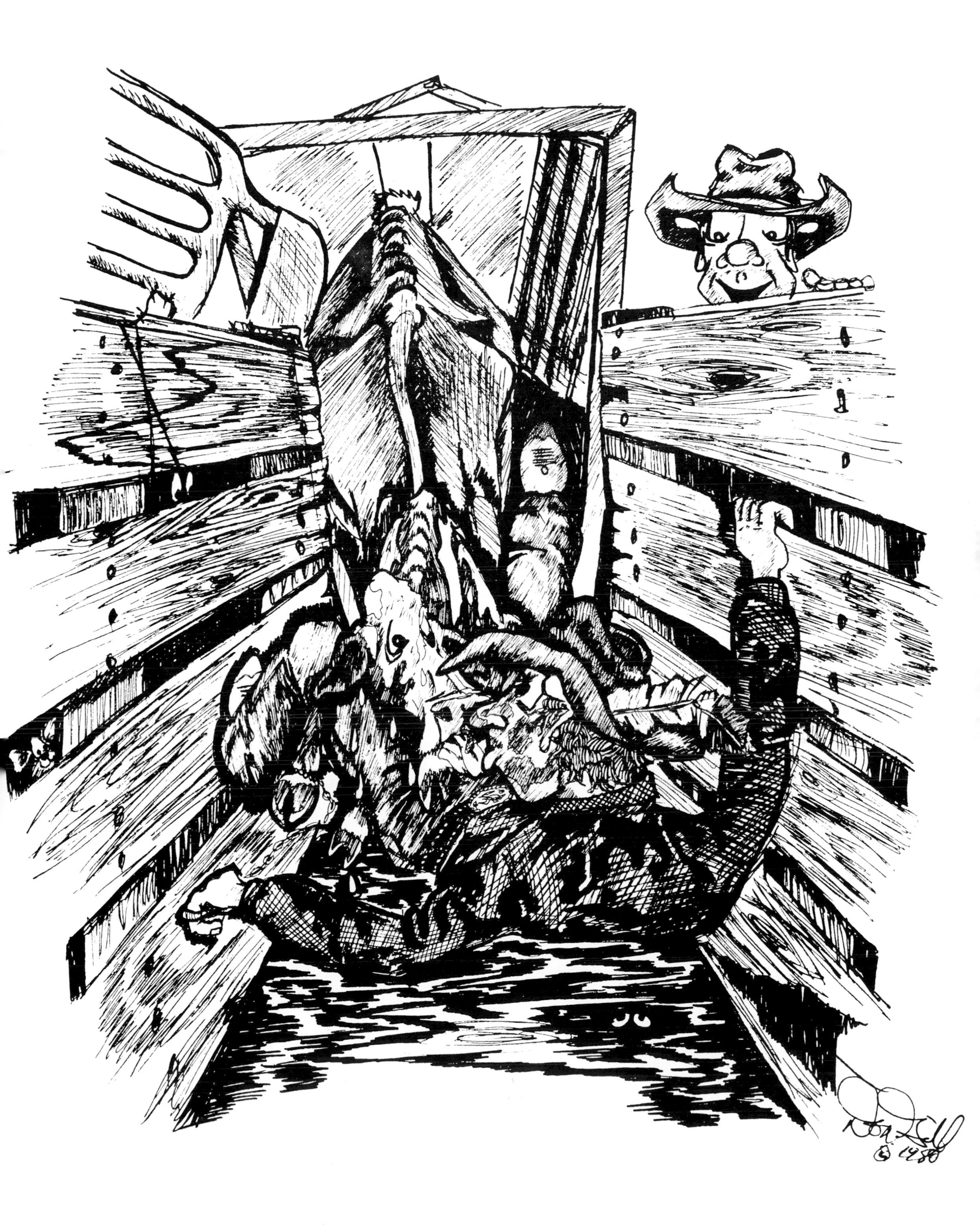

IT AIN'T EASY BEIN' A COWBOY

It ain't easy bein' a cowboy
like the Marlboro man
'Cause the public expects us
to all be from Texas
And roll cigarettes with one hand.
an' I don't even smoke!

Hollywood painted a picture
they like to perpetuate
The streets of Laredo
still echo his credo
That a cowboy always shoots straight.
an' I can't hit the broad side of a buffalo!

Then Nashville improved on the image
so now a cowboy can be
An illegal alien
like Willie and Waylien
Or a soap opera retiree.
an' I can't even sing!

I envy that smooth urban cowboy
whose dance card always seems full
I'd almost be willin'
to take penicillin
Or ride the mechanical bull.
'cause I'm tired of kissin' my horse!

It's hard to compete with Casey Tibbs,
Louie L'Amor and John Wayne
When the best that you've done
is a buckle you won
Worn smooth since that youthful campaign.
now I can't read without glasses!

The twentieth century cowboy,
what I'm supposed to be;
That rare combination
of civilization
And Jessie James on a spree.
but like I said . . .

It ain't easy bein' a cowboy
so I've made myself a vow
To avoid inspection
and public rejection
I'll jes' stay out here . . . with the cows.
hell, if it was easy, I'd be somethin' else!

TEX
BOB BLACK

TALK ABOUT TOUGH!

I've listened to you varmints braggin'
'Bout cowboys, the toughest you've known,
But the first liar don't have a chance, boys,
'Cause I knew one tough to the bone.

He came out from someplace in Kansas
In truth he was hard to dislike,
'Cause he weren't really mean, just hard headed.
They called him Peewilliker Mike.

When the weather got down below freezin'
Why, he'd never cover his ears.
So now each one looks like a knothole
'Cause pieces broke off through the years.

A she-bear invaded his camp once,
Insisted on sharin' his plate.
He saved the last of his biscuit
Though now he can jes' count to eight.

He used to have both of his elbows,
A forehead without so much slope,
'Til a cow jerked him outta the saddle . . .
He wouldn't let go of the rope.

He's faster than most fixin' fences
Though it's almost beyond belief,
'Cause he keeps both hands free fer poundin'
By stretchin' the wire with his teeth.

And what's more he don't use a hammer!
Drives nails with the back of his hand.
But this last thing I'm fixin' to tell ya
Will prove that there's no tougher man.

While pushin' a cow to the home ranch
Adrift in a cowboy's dreams,
A rattlesnake up and surprised him,
His horse came apart at the seams!

He bucked clean outta the saddle
So high that his bad breath condensed,
An' come down a cussin' and lighted
Astraddle a dang bob wire fence.

It cut'im right up to the buckle
Between his feet and his chin,
He jes' let his stirrups out longer
And rode his ol' pony on in.

Jan Swan Gifford
5/86 ©

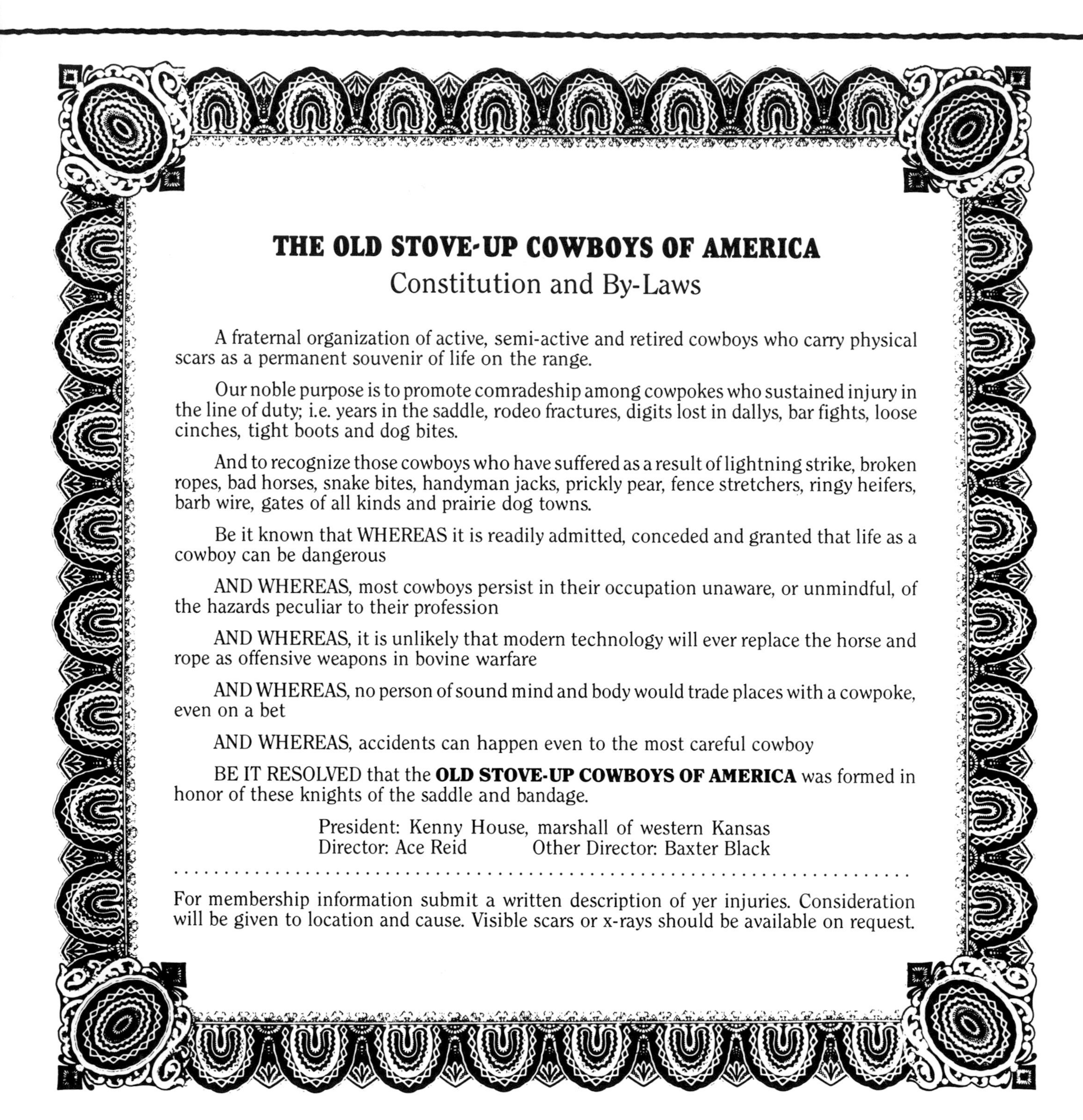

THE OLD STOVE-UP COWBOYS OF AMERICA
Constitution and By-Laws

A fraternal organization of active, semi-active and retired cowboys who carry physical scars as a permanent souvenir of life on the range.

Our noble purpose is to promote comradeship among cowpokes who sustained injury in the line of duty; i.e. years in the saddle, rodeo fractures, digits lost in dallys, bar fights, loose cinches, tight boots and dog bites.

And to recognize those cowboys who have suffered as a result of lightning strike, broken ropes, bad horses, snake bites, handyman jacks, prickly pear, fence stretchers, ringy heifers, barb wire, gates of all kinds and prairie dog towns.

Be it known that WHEREAS it is readily admitted, conceded and granted that life as a cowboy can be dangerous

AND WHEREAS, most cowboys persist in their occupation unaware, or unmindful, of the hazards peculiar to their profession

AND WHEREAS, it is unlikely that modern technology will ever replace the horse and rope as offensive weapons in bovine warfare

AND WHEREAS, no person of sound mind and body would trade places with a cowpoke, even on a bet

AND WHEREAS, accidents can happen even to the most careful cowboy

BE IT RESOLVED that the **OLD STOVE-UP COWBOYS OF AMERICA** was formed in honor of these knights of the saddle and bandage.

President: Kenny House, marshall of western Kansas
Director: Ace Reid Other Director: Baxter Black

. . . .

For membership information submit a written description of yer injuries. Consideration will be given to location and cause. Visible scars or x-rays should be available on request.

Hi Baxter:

I would like to join the Old Stove-Up Cowboys of America.

Permanent scars:

1 broken leg — left one — chasing cows.

1 broken arm — left one — chasing cows.

1 broken nose — standing too close.

Several not so bad scars.

Thank you,
Louis Luges
Vida, Montana

THE GAY CABELLERO

He wore a black hat and come up from Nevada
Ridin' a stockin' leg horse.
He was lookin' for work and he liked punchin' cattle,
In a manner of speakin', o' course.

He asked for a smoke and looked right at me
So I offered the makin's to him.
He took one look and politely refused;
He smoked only Virginia Slims.

He claimed he was a reata man
And he wore only west Texas boots.
He said that he never let meat touch his lips
His real preference was fruits.

He wore a bright kerchief and a gold-plated chain
With a locket attached, hangin' down.
I saw the inscription on the picture inside,
It said, "With all my love, Leroy Brown."

Now a cowboy don't usually ask questions
It's best to let sleeping dogs lie
But then he said he'd sleep in the bunk house
And gave me the wink of an eye.

He told me he didn't like violence.
He didn't like people with guns.
Then he asked me who was my hairdresser
And said I had cute little buns!

Now these cowboy jobs' hard to come by
Not something I'd easy dismiss
But I never thought twice about leavin'
When he puckered and blew me a kiss!

Later they said the boss hired him.
As a matter of fact, in my place!
But when they told me he was an actor
I began to get red in the face!

I realized I had been taken.
I'm bummin' while he's got my job.
He's eatin' corn in the cookhouse
I'm left chewin' the cob!

So tomorrow I'll look for employment
If they say they got nothin' in sight,
I'll play the gay cabellero
'Cause I'm wearin' my little pink tights!

Lory

WOMEN AND MULES

He's got a black hat and he's broke
He's lean as a bicycle spoke
    The fire in his eyes
    It ain't no surprise
He's a cowboy, that ain't no joke

If yer lookin' fer help, he's fer hire
He'll spur that bronc down to the wire
    Or break him to ride
    And rope either side
But don't ask him to sing in the choir

He's no good with a wrench in his hand
At milkin' or plowin' up land
    But give him a rope
    A horse at a lope
His purpose you'll soon understand

He camps out some nights on the ground
He's no good at settlin' down
    If it don't seem fair
    He'll say he don't care
Say, Bossman, I'll see you around

And ladies, he's usually bad news
He's good for a case of the blues
    But with a guitar
    In a smokey ol' bar
He'll charm you right out of your shoes

To scope him you don't need a key
Just remember he'll always be free
    If that's good enough
    Then it shouldn't be tough
Ya pretty much git what ya see

He plays kinda loose with the rules
And hardput to tolerate fools
    But he's good with a horse
    And children, of course
But he's hell on women and mules

Harry was a cowboy all his life. I don't mean no pickup drivin', two way radio talkin', Marlboro smokin', team ropin', bee boppin', baseball cap cowboy . . . I mean a real cowboy.

LOOKIN' BACK

All my life I been eatin' trail dust, punchin' cows and sleepin' in a bedroll.

I washed my socks in the river a million times and stunk so bad I smelled like an old beaver hide.

My feet's been froze and my head's been baked, I've growed enough hide over rope burns to cover ten saddles.

There's been times in my life I'd have give every dime I had for a dry boot.

I guess I've rode three or four hundred horses into the ground; some good, some not so good.

I've knowed an equal number of men; some good. But I thank whatever God watches over me that I've known at least one good woman.

I've probably lost more spurs, wore out more ropes, drunk more bad coffee and more good whiskey than most men.

I've eat them damn beans and chewed that tough meat 'til hell wouldn't have it.

I been hungry and tired, cold and broke, and there's been times I was ten miles from camp dyin' for a smoke and not a match in my pocket.

But I've been happy. Lord, that sun comin' up over the edge of the canyon, the chill comin' off the sage, that first cup of coffee 'fore you saddle up.

You couldn't buy that from me with fancy cars or easy chairs or PhD's.

This earth's give me a fair shake so far, but I don't see many young fellers followin' my footsteps.

But, by God, if some green buckaroo wants to make a hand someday I say more power to him!

I left him an easy trail to follow.

To my friend Harry Johnson who died January 10, 1981. Harry, I'm a better man for knowin' ya.

TALK ABOUT THE WEATHER

I've been out on JP Point one spring after the thaw
The water was so thick the fish could walk.
The road was washed out all the way but still I struggled on
Just drove my pickup truck from rock to rock.

And one time up at Grouse Creek it hailed all one day
Then I swear it settled into snow.
We had to dig a tunnel to put cows in the chute
And that's the day I froze off all my toes!

And then down at the Bare Ranch, the fog it was so thick
We didn't need a fence to hold'em in.
We gathered up some 2 by 8's and nailed'em to the air
And hung the gate securely on the end.

At Clipper Flats or Rafter T, I can't remember which
The weather turned off mighty cold indeed.
The wind come blowin' up and got the whip and chill
Right down to minus 99 degrees!

But if you're lookin' fer a hole to send someone you hate
Try the sheep corrals at Cat Creek by the rise.
The only place I ever stood in mud up to my knees
And had the dadgum dust blow in my eyes!

THE BIG HIGH AND LONESOME

The big high and lonesome's a place in my mind
like out from Lakeview to Burns.
Or up on the Judith or at Promontory
'bout where the U P track turns.
It's anywhere you feel tiny
when you get a good look at the sky
And sometimes when it's a'stormin'
you can look the Lord in the eye.

I stood and watched in amazement
out on San Augustine Plain
While the sky turned as black as the curtains in Hell
and the wind come a'chasin' the rain.
And standing there watching I felt it
in the minutes before it arrived
An unearthly stillness prickled my skin
like the storm itself was alive.

When it hit, it hit with a fury
the wind with its sabre unsheathed
Led the charge with the scream of a demon;
the storm was barin' its teeth.
The thunder cracked and the sky split apart
with a horrible deafening roar
I felt like a fox in a cage made of bones
in sight of the hounds at the door.

The blackness shook like a she-bear.
The lightning blinded the sun
The rain fell like bullets around me
scattering dust like a gun!
It was over as quick as it started
leaving it peaceful instead
The only sound was the beat of my heart
pounding inside of my head.

I took off my hat too shaken to move
afraid of making a sound
I felt like a man on the head of a pin
with nobody else around.
But the sun was already sparkling
in raindrops still wet on my face.
The big high and lonesome is only God's way
of putting a man in his place.

WHY DO THE TREES ALL LEAN IN WYOMING?

He said, "The wind never blows in Wyoming."
I said, "Mister, where you from?
It'll take the top offa big R.C.
Or peel an unripened plum!

Wherever you been, you been lied to!
I lived in Wyoming, I know.
I once seen a horse turned clean inside out
From standin' outside in a blow!

You don't have to shave in the winter.
Just pick a cool, windy place.
Stand there a minute, yer whiskers'll freeze
And break off next to yer face!

They claim that a boxcar in Rawlins,
A Denver and ol' Rio Grande,
Was picked off the tracks and blowed to the east
And beat the whole train to Cheyenne.

Why, they tell of a feller in Lander
Who jumped off a bale of hay
Before he hit ground the wind picked'im up
He came down in Casper next day!

They don't have to shear sheep in Worland
When they're ready, they wait for a breeze
And bunch'em in draws where the willers are thick
Then pick the wool offa the trees!

But the windiest tale that I heard
Was about the small town of Sinclair.
It used to set on the Idaho line
Then one spring it just blew over there!

I carry this rock in my pocket
For good luck and here's one for you.
Every little bit helps in Wyoming.
If yer skinny you better take two!

Well, stranger, you might just be part right.
Though, fer sure you ain't seen Devil's Tower.
Let's say the wind never blows in Wyoming . . .
Under eighty-five miles an hour!"

Don Hill
1982

HIGH TIDE IN WYOMING

They say that was a wet one
The spring of eighty-three
A feller out in Reno
Found a fish up in a tree.

Evinrude has built a store
In Lubbock by the sea
A man in Goodland, Kansas's
Sellin' beach front property.

They are shrimpin' in Nebraska
North Platte's struck off-shore oil
Pendleton's an island
Complete with sandy soil.

Rapid City's now a seaport
There's seaweed in Ouray
There's a Naval Base in Guymon
Or so the sailors say.

Out in Livingston, Montana
They export lobster tails
And Greenpeace moved to Provo
To protect the Utah whales.

They're growin' oysters down in Phoenix
There's a pier in Santa Fe
You can sail from California
Plum to Des Moines, Ioway.

I'm just tellin' what they told me
If you don't believe it's true
You better roll your pants up
Because I'm not quite through.

You may think I'm tellin' stories
And exaggerate a heap
But when it's high tide in Wyoming
You know it's gettin' deep.

DRYPOT MERCANTILE
GOODLAND, KS.
SORRY, WE'RE
OPEN
BOB BLACK

COW SAVVY

She's a ringy ol' bag with fire in her eyes
Some even say that she's smart
But true conversation with one of her kind
Is the height of a cowboy's art.

This four-legged baggage of hooves, horns and hair
Was put on this earth for one thing
To test every cowpunchin' buckaroo's salt
And see how much rawhide he swings.

Some claim she's so stupid she'll walk off a cliff
Or eat 'til she bloats up and dies
Sull up and pout like an indignant wife
Or drink water that's plum alkalized.

But the Lord in his wisdom gave her a foe
As worthy as any on earth
He's just as bullheaded and locoed sometimes
A hand from the day of his birth.

He'll slip up and rope her and break her to lead
By whippin' or draggin' by force
And just when he thinks he's figgered her out
She'll up and run under his horse.

Or if he's afoot just to doctor her calf
She paws and bellows and rants
Blows snot in his pocket, runs up his back
And leaves tracks on the seat of his pants.

She'll kick when she can and smash his ol' fingers
And never make him a dime
Tear down corrals, get choked in the chute
And go out the wrong gate every time.

It's a cowpuncher's lot to be stuck with the cow
As it says in the ballads they sing
They spend all their time outsmarting each other
You can't tell either a thing.

The only conclusion 'bout cowboys and critters
I've made, and I think that it's true
Is they're both so dang smart or both so dang dumb
But they both have the same size IQ.

There's probably more smooth tongued cows on the rangelands of the western states than anywhere else in the world. They get that way from tryin' to lick a grain or two of NaCl off that good ol' red rock salt.

After considerable deliberation I figger that the fellers that use that ol' rock salt do it for sentimental reasons.

THAT GOOD OL' RED ROCK SALT

It's May and I'm out packin' rock salt
The boss said to get it up high.
I been packin' all day with a couple o' mules
An a balface that's got a blue eye.

He got this salt on a bargain.
Laid in at twenty-two bucks.
It's reddish an' harder'n granite.
I'm wishin' them cows lots o' luck!

Cause the chance of a cow ever lickin'
A teaspoon o' salt off this load
Is the same as her lickin' the white
Off the inside of my ol' commode!

It's blowed outta salt mines in Utah
In chunks as big as yer head!
It erodes as slow as the Rockies,
Unweathered by storms overhead.

But I'm thinkin' whilst ridin' ol' piebald
This job ain't as bad as I feared.
'Cause I've come to the happy conclusion
You just put out salt once a year!

Those pieces of good ol' red rock salt
Just stand like a statue of stone
As the cows and the cowboys grow older
'Til we're nothin' but leather an' bone.

I reckon it's good fer the value.
I can't blame the boss, it's his dime.
It's cheap and, I'm sure, lasts forever
And that's SOMETHIN' in this day and time!

300 BC
1992 ©

EVOLUTION OF THE RANCH WIFE

October **(NEWLYWEDS)**
"Honey, the boys and I will be workin' cows all day. It's dangerous and dirty, especially for a pretty little thing like you. We'll be up to the house at noon. I'd sure appreciate it if you could fix us some lunch. There'll only be five of us but if you need help don't hesitate to call my mother."

April **(MARRIED 3 YRS)**
"Emily Jean, you stand behind that barrel. Sometimes these heifers get feisty after they calve. Once I get her tied down you hand me those chains and the calf puller. Be careful, Darlin', it's heavy."

July **(MARRIED 6 YRS)**
"Emily, sugar, the hayin' crew will be in at lunch time. I think there's 12 of 'em. I don't wanna stop this mornin' so when you bring out the coffee and sweetrolls at 9:30 would you mind just catchin' up to each baler and give it to the driver on the run. By the way, the tax man will be here at one o'clock. Take care of him, will ya?"

November **(MARRIED 10 YRS)**
"Emily, you sure you got that chain hooked good enough? Let the clutch out easy. When you feel the tractor starting to lug, drop to a lower gear and go slow. I don't want to lose any bales off the back of the pickup. Just follow the tracks. When we get out to the cows, I'll trade you. You can toss the bales and I'll drive. You wanna borrow my slicker?"

September **(MARRIED 13 YRS)**
"Em, crawl under here and hold this nut. I'll get up under the hood and turn the bolt from above. Watch out for that grease spot."

May **(MARRIED 17 YRS)**
"Mother, you spray the fly dope and keep the blackleg gun full. I'll rope'em. Junior and Jenny can help you flank the big calves."

October **(MARRIED A LONG TIME)**
"Ma, we're running' outta cows! Push 'em up!"

March **(NOT LONG AGO)**
"Dang it. I checked the heifers at midnight. It's your turn."

DEER John
WHOA
TERESA Schleigh
© 1986

THE SILENT PARTNER

Her name's on the note at the PCA, boys,
Though she might have questioned the loan
She signed her John Henry 'neath yours on the line
And she will 'til the kids are all grown.

Nobody's counted the pickups she's pulled
Or measured the miles she's put on the rake
Kept track of the pancakes or lunches she's packed
Or the number of times she lay there awake

Praying her prayers for the man in her bed.
God only knows, 'cause He's keepin' track.
She's buildin' up interest somewhere down the line
To use in a trade on your first cardiac.

She puts up with cows she knows you should cull
Scourin' calves on the livin' room floor,
Tracks in the bathroom and mud on the sheets,
Flies in the kitchen from broken screen doors.

She patiently listens to stories you tell
Recounting the skill of your blue heeler mate.
She wishes, herself, if that dog was so smart
You could teach that pot licker to open a gate!

She offers opinions that seldom sink in
'Til time, oft' as not, proves she was right.
But it's damn hard to figger how she could'a known?
You're not the only one who worries at night.

She's old as the mountain and young as the spring
Timeless in labor and wisdom and love.
Of all of God's creatures that man gets to share
The wife of a cowman was sent from above.

So lay there tonight when you go to bed.
Remember your partner, she's tried and she's true.
You're lucky, my man, to have such a friend
Take care of er, 'cause she takes care of you.

A RIDER, A ROPER AND A HELL'UVA WINDMILL MAN

Have you ever been out checkin' cows and makin' windmill rounds
In late November right after a snow?
And up against the fence line and piled in the draws
Drifts are humped up, clouds are hangin' low.

The wind cuts through your jacket and your seat upon the horse
Is the only part of you that's kinda warm.
You been all through the pasture and you haven't seen a cow
Then lookin' back up north you see the storm.

You look down in the bottom from your perch upon the rise
And hear the cows a'bawlin' 'fore you see
It don't take long to figger, that damn windmill's goin' wild
The pin's sheared off, the blades are spinnin' free.

You fight your way up through the bunch and see the water tank.
It's dry except for half an inch of ice.
You cock your head up skyward whil'st holdin' on yer hat
And what you see makes any man think twice.

The sucker rod has dropped down on the casing all the way.
My trouble's just beginnin', I can see.
The pin has broke in two and the gears have slipped theirselves
And the brake has come unhooked, oh, mercy me!

So I start up that ol' ladder with the rungs all slick with ice,
My big ol' clumsy mittens on my hands.
I'm steppin' mighty careful 'cause this windmill's real old
And there ain't no doctor waitin' in the stands.

I'm inchin my way up where I intend to catch the brake
And the sound I hear sends shivers down my track.
It's the scream of someone dyin' or a railroad train up close
Or a rabbit when you shoot and break his back.

It's the blades of that ol' windmill just a'singin' in the wind.
It's scary, brother, and I can tell you that!
I poke up through the platform just to take a little peek
And the vane comes swingin' round and swats my hat.

Then I get up there behind it and I'm hangin' on fer life.
It's the only time you'll ever hear me pray.
And any windmill ridin' cowboy'll tellya, it's fer sure
He'd rather ride a mustang any day!

I start back down to set the brake and on the thirteenth rung
The nails pull theirselves outt'a the pine.
I slip and fall through twelve, and then eleven, come on ten!
And catch myself when I hit number nine.

I'm shakin' when I hit the ground and try the brake real slow.
It works, oh, hallelujah, saved again.
But I got to git down to the shop and bring the pulley back
To pull the rod and get another pin.

I'll git'er fixed this evening and the cows'll be content.
I'll check the other windmills ridin' in.
And hope they'll all be workin' like Aeromotor says they should,
I don't think I can go through this again.

I've worked a lot of ranches where the windmill reigned supreme.
They might be testy like a pregnant wife
Or good as gold and never give a man a minute's pain,
But I've never seen a new one in my life!

Nothin' gives me greater pleasure than a windmill workin' right;
An oasis in the middle of an island.
Some may stop and praise its bounty, pumpin' water every pull
But me, why I just ride on by, a'smilin'.

(The best you could say about a cowboy down on the Pecos was, "He's a rider, a roper and a hell'uva windmill man!")

SANDHILLS SAVIOR

In the sandhills of Nebraska stands a monument of wills
Where man has staked his claim to them blowin', rollin' hills
Where the buffalo once scattered in the bunch grass, belly deep,
A whiteface calf, contented, sucks his mama, half asleep.

But you cannot know the beauty or appreciate the past
Unless you know the reason cows could stay and man could last.
For humankind is greedy and the babies need to eat
So to the rancher-farmer fell the task of growin' meat.

The fertile black dirt farmland runnin' up and down the Platte
Got covered up with people, their driveways and their cat
And them that lived in cities saw no use for sandhills land
So the cattlemen and cowboys come up north to try their hand.

They treated her with reverence and learned what Indians knew
That it cannot take abusin' 'cause she's fragile through and through
And they learned a crucial factor to keep them cows alive
Takes more than snow and sunlight, it takes water to survive.

So they dug their dainty windmills and pumped life outta the ground
It allowed the cows to flourish so the people stayed around
Then little townships prospered and, you can see by now,
They've built a whole existence upon the humble cow.

From Thedford to Hyannis, from Valentine to Rose
Across that sandy country where the prairie grass still grows
You'll see those man-made daisies, silhouettes against the sky
Their steel petals gleaming on their stalks eighteen feet high.

On Nebraska highway twenty or state road eighty-three
There's a million creakin' windmills standin' proud for you to see.
They represent a people and the land they're livin' in
The lifeblood of the sandhills spinnin' freely in the wind.

1982

WORKIN' COWS DOWN TO MALTA

We wuz down to Malta last fall jus' when the first cold spell come in. I'm tellin' you, when it's cold, it is damn sure cold in Malta! Wind blows across there, well, for sure it wuz nineteen degrees, the wind was blowin' twenty in gusts to thirty five. Talk about a whip an' chill factor!

We wuz workin' some light heifers up, runnin'em through the squeeze chute and freezin' to death! I wuz on one side givin' the shots, Tinker and Gus wuz on t'other workin' the chute, it was a Powder River. Boy, we froze there fer 'bout an hour and a half when somebody sez, "Hey, whyn't we build a little fire."

So we all went around and gathered up a bunch of tumbleweeds, lit'er on fire, set a big blaze that went twenty foot in the air and burned to the ground in a minute and a half.

We stopped everything! We made a little search party an' went out to gather some wood. We come back with pieces of post, lumber, baler twine and ol' boards and lit'em up.

Of course, Gus, ya know, built the fire right up wind from the chute. It wuz a real dandy. The smoke jus' pourin' in on us. Well, he wuddn't satisfied with the nice little fire we had goin' so he went out an' here he come back with big ol' truck tire which he proceeded to throw right on top of the fire and held it down with a three foot piece of creosote tie!

'Bout five minutes that tire caught fire and the black smoke come boilin' outta there!

The wind, o'course, was blowin' so hard it never let the smoke git above eye level. Blowin' in right across the chute where we's all tryin' to work.

We're all blacker'n pitch and covered with soot. You couldn't see nobody, much less recogniz'em. Ol' Bob Lightfoot spit out his cigarette, wiped the black off his eyes so's he looked like a raccoon and said, "I feel jus' like a smoked ham!"

THE DEAD COW RANCH

Bubba and Billy Bob grew up together. From grade school on. They's best of friends. Now Billy Bob was one of them fellers who had the "King Midas touch." Everything he touched turned to gold. Bubba, on the other hand; everything he touched turned to sheep pellets! Billy Bob was the class valedictorian, captain of the football team and Twirp King. Bubba never graduated.

Well, they both went into the cow business and married up. Billy Bob's success continued. He payed off the loan the first year on his cows. In five years he owned his place free and clear. To this day Bubba has NEVER owned a cow free and clear! Matter of fact, in 1965 Bubba changed the name of his ranch. He called it the Dead Cow Ranch. This was his brand:

He called it Tits up!

Twenty years later Billy Bob's luck is still holdin' true. He's gotta nice place and a fine young son he called Billy Bob Junior. Bubba is still draggin' along, toughin' it out and he has a beautiful daughter named Wava Dean.

Bubba came home late one evenin' on one of them cold, windy March days. Where the flag looks like it's ironed against the sky. He'd been workin' on a calvy heifer since noon; pulled the three point hitch off the tractor, broke three log chains and tore the frame outta the barn door. He sat down at the table in his usual despair. He reached around behind the gun case where he always kept a big jug of 'grape Nehi.' He's a suckin' on that jug when his darlin' wife come to the kitchen door.

"Bubber, honey, I gotta talk to ya 'bout somethin'."

"Can't you see I'm wore out . . . Jus' let me set a minute . . ."

"Bubber, it's important. It's about our daughter, Wava Dean. You know our daughter?"

" 'Course I know'er! She's been livin' here nineteen years! You're probably gonna tell me she's in the 'family way'."

"Oh, Bubber, I'm sorry to say it, that's right!"

"Dadgummit! I mighta known! And I know who did it, too. Billy Bob's boy!"

He jumped outta the chair, run out and leaped in the pickup, threw gravel all over the front porch and peeled over to Billy Bob's ranch. 'Course the pickup broke down at the cattle guard and he had to walk all the way up the lane. Lost both five buckles. His luck was runnin' true.

Now Billy Bob seen him comin' up the drive and met him at the door.

"Come in, Bubba, I know all about it. I talked to my boy and I know why yer here. I'm gonna do all I can to make it right. Set down and have a drink."

He poured him a big ol' shot of . . . grape Nehi.

"Now let me tellya what I'm gonna do. Tomorrow I'll take them kids down and buy'em a big diamond ring. We'll make the announcement and hav'em a big wedding. I'll pay fer it all. Then I'm gonna set up a hundred thousand dollar trust fund fer that child."

All this time Bubba ain't sayin' nuthin.' Just settin' there with that ol' sour look on his face; little purple slobbers on his chin.

"Then, I tell you what, you and I will go out and find a nice little ranch fer'em and I'll make the down payment. Then together we'll spot'em a hundred good cows, I'll cosign the note. We'll giv'em a start like you and I never had."

Bubba still ain't said nothin.' Just settin' there drippin' all over the front of his shirt. Finally Billy Bob says, "What's the matter with you, Bubba? These things happen and I'm doin' my best to make it right! Ain't you got nothin' to say?"

Bubba looked up at his ol' pardner and said, "Billy Bob, can we bring'er back if she ain't settled?"

THE COW COMMITTEE

Once upon a time
 At the start of all creation
Angels sat upon a cloud.
 An odd conglomeration
Of buckaroos from near and far
 But not there from the city.
Their job; to build a brand new beast.
 They were the Cow Committee.

"Now me, I'd like some floppy ears,"
 Suggested Texas Jake.
"Floppy ears would freeze plum off
 On the Powder or the Snake!"
"Up north we need some curly hair,"
 Said Colorado Bill,
"Hide that's tight and hair that's thick
 To ward against the chill."

"Hold yer horses, one and all,"
 Said Omaha Eugene,
"Nebraska needs a fleshy cow;
 A real corn machine!"
"She'd waste away!" cried Tucson Bob,
 "What we need's a hump.
One who'll live on tumbleweeds
 And run from clump to clump."

"How 'bout horns?" said Oakdale Pete.
 "Don't need'em in Des Moines."
"We'll make some with and some without
 And some with tenderloins."
"Some with sheaths that drag the grass
 And some so dadgum tall
To hear her calf down on the ground
 She'd have to place a call!"

"I'd like'm roan," said Shorthorn Mike.
 "No, black," said Angus Tink.
"White or red," said Hereford Hank,
 "I'd even take'm pink!"
"Whatever suits you tickles me,"
 Said Juan from Mexico.
"I second that," said Crossbred Jack,
 "Just make'm so they grow."

They made some white. They made some blue.
 They made some orange and spotted.
They never made a green one
 But they made'm tall and squatted.
In every shape and every size
 But no one had decided
How to make the perfect cow;
 On that they were divided.

This went on for days and days,
 In fact, it never ended.
Each time they reached some middle ground
 The project was amended.
They still meet from time to time
 And argue with their leaders.
The Cow Committee carries on. . .
 They're now the purebred breeders.

illustrated by Charles Marsh, the Farm Journal.

THE KEEPER OF THE KEY

There's a strange group of people who speak in sacred tongues.
They gather in convention halls and really test their lungs.

And to those on the outside, they're god-like and they're wise
As they try to win a convert with passion in their eyes.

They begin to speak of bloodlines, of cows their bull has sired
With evangelistic reverence, they truly are inspired.

Recounting her performance and weight per day of age
They rattle off her record reciting page on page.

Her progeny's outstanding. Their birth weight's sure to please.
She's ranked above the average in rel'tive calving ease.

She might be black or Brahmer, Gelbvieh, Maine Anjou,
Simmental or Santa, just to name a few

Herefords, polled or muley, some foreign soundin' name.
It doesn't make much difference, the story's all the same.

They breed the purebred cattle and know their cows by heart.
And they'll talk yer dang fool leg off, if you let'em start!

But I got to give'm credit 'cause resting in their hand
Is the blueprint of the future for cows throughout the land.

So I'll try to learn the business; call a bull by name
But I've made one observation 'bout people in this game;

Listenin' to these purebred folks makes me think right now
New Delhi's not the only place they have a sacred cow!

SHOW BARN
1982

CROSSBRED STEW

The steer that topped the show this year was partly Chianina.
The bull that threw the biggest calf was partly Simmental.
The carcass class was swept away by three-eighths Limousiners
The Gelbvieh cross was judged the best in this year's overall.

The feedlot men like Piedmontese to feed as crossbred critters
Or any kind of cloven hoof that shows some part Charolais.
A Salers cross or Tarentaise that's half or quarter blooded
Or maybe half breed Longhorn calves or partly Murray Grey.

The Brahman breeders took a bull and made Santa Gertrudis
They built a Brangus with a cross and found out what to do.
They stirred the pot a couple times and made Beefmaster heifers.
Descendants of BOS INDICUS are now cross brahmer stew.

We like exotic crosses in the feedlot and show ring.
What's happened to the Angus and their Hereford counterpart?
They may not get top billing though the question still remains
If they're only part exotic, then what's the other part?

KEYSTONE, CA / TAILED EIGHT, AZ / THIRTY SLASH, TX / COFFEE POT, TX / U DOT, NM / BRIDLE BIT, TX / Tijeras SCISSORS, NM
CIRCLE DOT, NM / COW'S HEAD, NE / SWING EASY, WY / LUCKY SEVEN, TX / DOUBLE TRIANGE, TX / ROCKING CHAIR, TX
RAFTER CROSS, NE / ARROW E, CA / HASH KNIFE, TX / FISH HOOK, AZ / SUNRISE, NM / COVERED STAR, NE

BEEF-A PHANTES
HYRAM-TEX
HAMPFORD's
IF THEY CAN'T EAT IT OR JUMP IT, THEY'L ROOT UNDER IT
DAD
MOM

BENTLEY THE BORN-AGAIN BULL

It was one of those two o'clock mornin' calls: "Looked like everything was comin' jes' fine, Doc, then he got stuck! Could you come?"

On the way out to the ranch I put the truck on autopilot while my foggy brain sifted through the possibilities. Hip lock, more than likely, I figgered. I walked into the calvin' barn, shook the snow off my coat and surveyed the scene. Fairly peaceful. Two unshaven cowboys playin' cards in front of the space heater and a good-sized heifer standing in the chute looking no worse for the wear. "Good," I thought, "The boys haven't worn the heifer out before they called." Or themselves either, for that matter.

I peeled down to my shortsleeve coveralls and went to survey the battlefield. There, underneath the heifer's cocked tail, peering out at the new world was Bentley, the baby bull calf. All I could see was his head. With mama's help he'd gotten far enough to pop his nose and his ears out and no further. He didn't seem in distress, just a little embarrassed. He looked like some trophy hunter's prize hangin' on the den wall.

Since the umbilical cord hadn't broken yet he had no need to breathe but he was lookin' around like a kid in a neck brace at the county fair. After my examination I concluded he had one front leg into the birth canal and the other pointing straight back. He was wedged in tight as a new hat band.

"Bentley," I said, "I hope you brought your scuba gear because you've got to go back inside." I gave the heifer an epidural injection so she couldn't strain. I put my hand over his nose and started to push. Bentley raised an eyebrow and looked up at me. "You sure you've got a license to do this?" he said. "Sure," says I, "I bought it from a guy in Iowa when he sold out his practice!"

It wasn't easy, but I popped the little duffer back in, straightened his legs and then pulled him into the outside world.

He was typically ungrateful as I rubbed him down and pointed him to the breakfast nook under mama's flank. He turned once and looked at me, "I've heard of being born again," he said, "but this is ridiculous!"

THE BARROOM DEAL

Sometimes the boss would make one of those "barroom deals." Like the time he bought Tex's cows (the names have been changed to protect the guilty).

Tex was one of yer genyoowine gypo cow traders and had injected a few loads of cows into us before. The boss told me it wouldn't be necessary to do much to the cows since Tex had assured him they were all young, sound and gar-on-teed bred.

Saturday morning, sun shinin', a beautiful spring day; we gathered on a hill near the small town of Murphy. Tex brought along a couple of exchange students from Chihuahua to help. He was none too pleased 'bout havin' to work these cows in the first place. He thought it suggested, somehow, that we were skeptical of his description of the cows' condition. That, and the fact that he had no corrals to work 'em in since he was just the middleman anyway.

Tex had built a temporary holding pen out of snow fence, chicken wire and steel posts. It looked like a concentration camp for discarded barnfowl. He'd rustled up some old panels and the first squeeze chute ever used by Thomas Jefferson. It was a Powder River squeeze and a Teco head gate. It was uniformly rust color and appeared to be held together by baler twine and botched welding beads.

The first cow clomped in and I put on a plastic sleeve to preg check her.

"Whattya doin'?" asked Tex.

"Whattya think I'm doin', measurin' her for a monacle?"

"They're all bred. My brother checked 'em last week. He kin tell by the way the hair lies on their spine."

The first one was open. As were the next seven. We worked for a couple hours, stoppin' to repair the chute twice. The cows were gettin' restless. Two of the boys stood on the ground between the chicken wire fence and the herd. They fended them off by shakin' a broken plastic whip and an empty Purina Dog Chow bag.

"This 'un's bound to be good," said Tex as he pushed a big, horned cow into the chute. She hit the head gate like a mortar shell just as I clamped the bar down over her neck. She never slowed down. She tore the head gate off and headed for the hills. The last time I saw her she was disappearin' over a creek bank followed by 172 head of "gar-on-teed" bovine reprobates. The head gate hung around her head like a picture frame. She was draggin' two miles of chicken wire, a 40-foot nylon rope and an empty bag of Purina Dog Chow.

The deal fell through. Sometimes we jes' git lucky.

ONE MORE YEAR

Every fall when I go out to preg check the cows I find a few that, so far as I'm concerned, need cullin'. So I point out the reasons in my best professional manner and cut her off to the side but that don't always seem to satisfy the cowboy runnin' the cows.

Now they wouldn't ever admit to likin' one of them ol' shells but they recall her better days and want'a make sure she's had every chance. So the conversation between the green young vet'inary and the experienced rancher goes somethin' like this . . .

WHAT'S THE STORY ON THAT GOOD OL' COW?
THE BOWLEGGED COWBOY ASKED.
She's sorta gimpy on the left hind leg
And her breathin's kinda fast.

SHUCKS! I REMEMBER WHEN SHE WUZ BORNED
IT WUDDN'T THAT LONG AGO.
Well, somebody bobbed her tail last year
But, hell, I guess you oughta know.

YOU BET YER LIFE! I KNOW THAT COW!
SHE'S AS GOOD A ONE AS I'VE SAW!
I jus' thought since she's gettin' thin
And gotta big lump on her jaw.

THAT AIN'T NOTHIN'! JUST A LITTLE KNOT!
THE BOWLEGGED COWBOY SAID.
Yeah, but one eye's blue and she leppied her calf
And she ain't gotta tooth in her head.

LISTEN KID, I 'MEMBER THAT COW!
WHY, I EVEN MILKED'ER FER AWHILE!
Sure but she's gotta swing bag an' one big tit
And skin like a crocodile!

KID! YOU GOTTA ADMIT SHE KNOWS THE RANGE
AND EVERY WATER HOLE!
I hate to tell you she's open now
And these prolapse stitches won't hold.

SHE'S NOTHIN' TO ME, DON'T GIT ME WRONG,
I KNOW SHE'S GETTIN' OLD,
Well, yer the boss, if you want'a keep her
Whatever you say goes

But if it'uz me I'd cull'er fast
And never shed a tear.
WELL. . .I GOTTA LITTLE GRASS OUT BEHIND THE HOUSE. . .
LET'S RUN HER ANOTHER YEAR.

SELLIN' PREWITT'S COW

Now these ol' boys that own sale barns have occasion to speculate on an ol' cow now and then. They buy her, feed her a week or two, then try and slip'er back through the sale. They get down in the ring to keep her good side to the crowd. They look up at the auctioneer and he begins:

Hey, bid alright, sir. . .step right up
we're gonna sell this fine cow.

I've got a 5 dollar bid on a cow,
a good cow, who'll give ten. . .
Walkin' on three, milkin' on two. . .
You ain't got ten I ain't through.

"Cause I'll take eight, give me eight. . .
This cow's great. . .
One big foot and one bad ear
What do you care if she can't hear!

Nothin' wrong that you can't fix. . .
You won't give eight, I'll take six!
Six big bills, c'mon try. . .
She don't need but one good eye.

What do you mean she ain't alive!
See her breathin'. . .I'll take five.
C'mon boys, you make me sore. . .
CALL THE VET. . .I'll take four!

Four ain't much, she' just a pup. . .
C'MON PREWITT, GIT'ER UP!
C'mon boys, nothin's free. . .
GIT THE TRACTOR. . .I'll take three!

Three is all I'm askin' now. . .
Surely someone needs this cow!
You may think that I'm all through. . .
There's still a chance. . .I'll take two!

PREWITT, GIT'ER PROPPED UP STRAIGHT. . .
LEAN'ER UP AGAINST THE GATE!
Fine replacement, bled and pregged. . .
Pay no mind to that bad leg.

She's a dandy, not too old. . .
Tits'll grow back so I'm told. . .
Rigor mortis?. . .No, just tense. . .
Someone give me 50 cents!

Anybody give a dime?
Hurry up! There ain't much time!
C'mon boys. . .use your head. . .
DAMMIT, PREWITT, NOW SHE'S DEAD!

R.A.

Attention, you gypos and traders
And gamblers whose lives are precarious.
You live to buy cows, in spite of yer vows
And resort to methods nefarious.

You sneak off to look for a herd sire.
You know what they ask is preposterous.
In spite of the price, you bid on him twice,
He's exotic . . . part hippopotamus!

You covet a set of bred heifers.
They're so cheap it's almost ridiculous.
There's nary a hint what's in the fine print,
They're bangers and also tuberculous.

The neighbor is sellin' his milk cow.
She's guaranteed bred and homogenous.
You buy her just right, she dies overnight,
Yer bad luck is gettin' monotonous.

If all of this sounds too familiar
Yer habit's become too precipitous.
Then please call on us before you go bust
And wind up becoming extinctofous.

We're reformed ex-stockers and cowmen
Who've sworn off that habit odiferous.
When cows make you drool call eight-two-two-fool,
We'll stop you from being impetuous.

When a bargain comes through at the sale
Yer tempted and think you need one of us . . .
Yer never alone, just pick up the phone,
We call ourselves Rancher's Anonymous.

FOLGERS
COFFE

A TIME TO STAY, A TIME TO GO

Ya know, I got this ranch from my daddy
He come here in seventeen.
He carved this place outta muscle and blood;
His own and his ol' 'percheon' team.

I took over in fifty
And married my darlin' in May.
Together we weathered whatever came up
She had what it took to stay.

Last winter we finally decided
We'd pack up and leave in the spring.
The kids are all grown and 'city-folk,' now;
We never raised'em to cling.

Oh sure, I wished they'd have wanted
To ranch and carry it on
But they did their part, I thank'em fer that
And they chose. Now all of 'em's gone.

The last thirty odd years we've collected
An amazing number of things!
Bonnets and bottles, clippings and letters
And Dad's ol' surcingle rings.

We've spent the winter months sorting.
Our hearts would ache or would jump
As we looked at our lives in trinkets we'd saved
Then boxed up or took to the dump.

We cried sometimes in the attic
I'm not ashamed of the truth.
I love this ol' ranch that we're leavin'
We gave it the strength of our youth.

I love this ol' woman beside me
She held me and stayed by my side.
When I told'er I's thinkin' 'bout sellin'
She said, "Honey, I'm here for the ride."

These new fellers movin' in Monday
Are nice and I wish'em good luck.
But I'd rather be gone, so Ma, git yer stuff
I've already gassed up the truck.

Lookin' back over my shoulder
At the mailbox I guess that I know
There's a time to be stayin', a time to be goin'
And I reckon it's time that we go.

CATTLEMAN'S PRAYER

"Lord, this dang cattle business gets me down sometimes. I really wanta stay in it. Way down deep I guess I feel like I'm doin' somethin' worthwhile; feedin' people, that is. I used to think I had a handle on the business. You know, the cycles, up then down, then up. Ride out the hard times 'cause the good times are comin'. But anymore I'm feelin' kinda uneasy.

I never figured on politics messin' up the cycles. Price freezes, boycotts, kangaroo meat, grain embargos, brucellosis regulations, animal welfare folks, the Delaney amendment, the no-meat diet; I wasn't expectin' these things. If I ever thought about them at all I sure never thought they'd cause much trouble.

I can operate in a business of supply and demand and take my chances. I'd gladly do it but give me some advice 'bout how to argue against naturopathic nutritionists who say meat is bad for you and against vegetarian veterinarians who say we mistreat livestock. Maybe it takes someone smarter'n me.

Lord, please don't think me ungrateful. I'm makin' the payments on a $14,000 pickup, Ma's got a microwave, the kids are healthy and the banker extended my loan. I'm thankful to live in these United States. Everywhere I've been in this country I can feel the freedom flowin' through our veins. *And* I've got the freedom to choose what I do for a livin'. I must like the cattle business or I'd be pumpin' gas or mowin' lawns, right?

I guess I'm just gettin' enough age on me now where I'm beginnin' to see that one feller, no matter how hard he tries, can't do it all himself. We need yer help. I reckon I'm prayin' for a way of life I don't want to see go down the drain.

I'm sorry I sound like I'm complainin' but I just had to tell somebody. Thanks for listenin'. Amen."

THE GAMBLER

When the corn's all gone to tassel in the Colorado fall
And the April future's crowdin' ninety cents,
An electric kinda feelin' gets to floatin' in the air
That makes you take your leave of common sense.

Them Texas calves look better than they ever have before.
You can buy'em now for eight cents on the dime.
And lay'em in the feedyard at under eighty-five.
They're ripe for pickin', boy, and now's the time.

So you call the order buyer and put him on the road.
You want to get'em 'fore the market peaks.
You tell the cattle foreman to get the crew in gear
And you fill'er up, eight thousand in two weeks.

They arrive in good condition for a thousand mile trip.
The weather's holdin' pretty much the same
And you finally get'em processed and started up on feed
Then, by gosh, it settles in to rain.

The pens that looked so pretty with the straw all scattered 'round
Become a quagmire; puddles, ponds and bogs.
The mud behind the feed bunk is gettin' ankle deep
Them calves look less like cattle, more like hogs.

It hangs all gray and cloudy as the days drip slowly by
'neath overcast November, sorry skies.
The cowboys' workin' overtime to pull the sick ones out
But they keep dyin', dyin' just like flies.

There ain't no magic potion, nothin' seems to work
The vet'inary's done pulled out his hair.
The crew is gettin' owly and fightin' with themselves
And lookin' back it just don't seem quite fair.

'Cause you had them cattle bought right, it really shoulda worked.
You didn't plan on losin' ten percent
Plus the fact May futures' down the limit once again
Plus all the time and money you have spent.

But then you say, "Aw, what the hell, tomorrow it might change.
There ain't no point in settin' here a'grievin'
If corn goes down to one O five and calves hit two fifteen
Then I may stand a chance of breakin'even!"

"The springtime winds'll dry me out, by summer I'll be healed
And ready for another free-fer-all.
'Cause I don't need Las Vegas, just a set of Texas calves
And Colorado weather in the fall."

KEEP ON TRUCKIN

THE PHANTOM ORDER BUYER

This fall I sat and watched in amazement
As the trucks come in to unload.

They bought 'em as #2 okies
And you can sure tell they been on the road.

Scattered amongst a few good ones
There's no tellin' what you might see

A collection of misfits and travelers
Who've been on the road since last spring

And them that ain't down are sure dandies,
Their tails a'draggin' the ground.

It must cost quite a bit to buy'em as beef
'Cause horns ain't worth much by the pound.

Now you can't blame all of the buyers
Or even some of 'em all of the time

'Cause when they buy one that's ten cents over
They buy a chronic to split the dime.

But there must be a phantom cow buyer
Who buys a lot of our calves

'Cause you'll never get ours to admit
That they ever bought one that's bad.

Now I don't know nothin' 'bout buyin'
And I ain't got no room to talk

But I'm sure their chance would be better
If, when you bought'em, they could still walk.

So in the words of my friend Glenn McQuilkin
It's nothin' but plain common sense.

Please buy the ones in the center of the ring
Not leanin' against the fence!

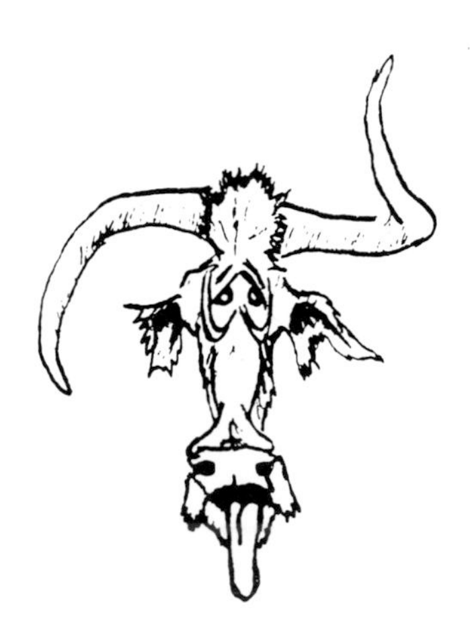

OH NO, IT'S GONNA GO HIGHER!

The market was so hot on Monday
The buyers were burnin' his door.
The cattle he'd bought for seventy cents
Were bringin' six bits, maybe more.

On Tuesday they went even higher
It was hard not to sell at that price
But he knew in his heart that tomorrow
He'd win, he was rollin' the dice.

On Wednesday they went through the ceiling
He'd never seen fats go so high.
But that afternoon they were slippin'
But that never worried our guy.

'Cause his broker and banker and guru
Had predicted the down slide was done
So at ten o'clock that Thursday morning
Our hero turned down eighty-one.

Friday broke dismal and dreary
The market continued to fall.
He watched it go down to breakeven
And not even one buyer called.

That weekend, consulting the paper,
His horoscope promised good news.
That was sure worth a drink at the Elks Club,
He got snockered plum out of his shoes.

Monday was gloomy, Tuesday was bad
The rest of the week it was worse.
By Friday the price of grain jumped up
And that just made him feel cursed.

By midweek he finally was offered
A sure bid of sixty-five cents.
But he held fast at sixty-five fifty
So the buyer packed up and went.

I know yer expectin' a moral
Explainin' the lessons he learned
'Bout the man who thinks higher and higher
Most likely gets his lower burned.

But there isn't no use to pretend
That a feeder or one of their kind
Would lock in a profit of eight cents, if
He thought he could hold out for nine.

And what of our hero, yer askin'?
I guess I kin tellya 'bout that.
He sold'em for sixty-two fifty
Then got docked for bein' too fat.

THE INSULT

Jimmy was so mad at ol' Billy
When he told me I thought he spit fire!
He said his mommy's a Holstein heifer
An' his daddy's a piece o' barb wire!

HIGH GOOD

The Holstein cross in a feedlot
Was often scorned and maligned.
Packer buyers would sort them off
Refusing all of their kind.

But time and grading standards
Have changed the Holstein's luck;
Now they're black belted Angus
And slip right onto the truck.

THE 20TH CENTURY RUSTLER

Oh; where have all of the rustlers gone
    That worked in the pale moonlight
And gathered our cattle while everyone slept
    Then split like a thief in the night?

Remington painted their dastardly deeds
    Preachers condemned them to hell
But twentieth century rustlers exist,
    They work for MBPXL!

From Iowa Beef or Armour and Swift
    They come to dicker and trade
The lone packer buyer, a scowl on his face,
    Telling you why they won't grade.

He's trained in his craft like others before
    Picking your pocket's his vice
He's learned all his tricks from the FAT BUYER'S GUIDE
    That keeps him from paying full price.

It lists all the reasons to discount your steers;
    They might be too fat or too thin,
Too many tags, need more days on the feed,
    Too many horns in the pen,

Too many left handed pitchers this year,
    Too many days in the week,
The phase of the moon, his barber's advice
    And, of course, the Yellow Sheet.

You can beg him to come see your heifers
    Plead with him on bended knee
Your calls go unanswered, the phone never rings,
    The ball's in his court, don't you see.

But sometimes the market is bullish
    They're lined up outside your door.
They promise you things will be different
    They won't even ask for a sort.

So you put him a small load together
    You pack 'til the semi is full.
A couple foot rots, a prolapsed old cow,
    The four year old highlander bull.

The hardwares, the brainers, the heifers in calf,
    You ship all the chronics to town.
They never complain, just chew their cigar
    'Cause they know the wheel goes around.

There are those who insist they can't be all bad
    So I'll close before I get hung.
Most packer buyers are living examples
    Why mothers of some eat their young!

MARK VI
WHERE'S
TH
BEEF
© '84

HI TECH PIG

What I know about pigs you could put in a hat
Except that they're friendly, fertile and fat
And frequently fried, I know about that.

They come in all sizes and colors and shapes
They show up on salads, in sausage and crepes
But, thankfully, 31 Flavors escapes.

We call them by names like Piglet and Hamp,
Hamlet, Clyde Barrow, Miss Piggy the Vamp
But none is more famous than Porky, the Champ.

I can boar y'all plenty 'bout fat back and rind
But I feel no gilt when praising their kind
Though often they're scoffed at, scorned or maligned.

'Cause pork belly futures and good BLT's,
Barbecued ribs or cold ham and cheese
Will keep 'em around, our palates to please.

For the sow has distinguished herself in a crate.
We control their environment, their mood and their fate,
So it takes less time to gain the same weight.

We've created high technological swine.
Genetically bred to save ground corn and time
And bright county agents have rations designed

That makes pigs grow faster'n a packin' house dog.
Prof's call it progress in their school catalogue
But the pig could care less . . . what's time to a hog?

GROWTH RATE TABLE
SHIP SATURDAY
200 lb. FRIDAY
150 lb. THURSDAY
100 lb. WEDNESDAY
50 lb TUESDAY
25 lb. MONDAY
SIMPLOT
STAND BACK! PIGS GROWING
PRODUCTION CHART
BOB BLACK

IT'S A DOG'S LIFE

It's a dog's life bein' a cat
Hangin' around the house.
Always on a diet.
You know how many calories in a mouse?

> You think it's easy bein' a cat?
> This'll make you laugh,
> I'll bet there ain't a human being
> Who can give himself a bath!

Some of them places is hard to reach
Especially if you're not too young!
But the worst of all the problems
Is gettin' that fur off yer tongue!

> They give us ridiculous names
> Like Foster or Lawrence or Percival.
> Call me fer dinner or fergit it!
> Those humiliatin' names are unmerciful!

I've heard of a cat named D Eight.
Heard of a cat bein' cool.
I've even heard of a cat house.
Must be some kind of a school.

> They never give you overshoes.
> They don't even give you socks.
> I wish you had to go barefooted
> An' use an ol' cat box!

It's a dog's life bein' a cat
Since this is the end of the story
I think I'll back up to the sofa
An' mark out my new territory.

> Therefore in final conclusion
> To my feline monologue
> I'll leave you with a little wisdom:
> Never trust a smiling dog!

CRACK!!
POP!!

RD
JAY
ADAMS
'86

RAININ' CATS & DOGS

You've no doubt heard that ol' sayin', "It's rainin' cats and dogs." Let me tell ya how that sayin' came about. Billy Bob was settin' in the house, coolin' his heels and watchin' ONE DAY AT A TIME when his darlin' wife said, "Billy Bob, that dang cat done clum up the poplar tree!"

Billy Bob 'splained how cats did that to get a better view and he'd be alright. Next day missus remarked how that dang cat was still up in the poplar tree. "He's liable to die up there," she said.

"Naw," said Billy Bob, "Cats don't die in trees. If they did we'd find bones in the firewood."

On the third day she made Billy Bob climb the tree to rescue the cat. He got about halfway up and the branches started breakin.' Them poplar trees grow straight up and the branches are brittle as a machine-made taco shell. He took a swipe at the cat who scratched him and climbed higher.

"Maybe you could shake him out,'" said Missus.

Billy Bob tied a rope as high in the poplar tree as he could and took a dally on his pickup bumper. He jerked the tree a few times but the cat just sunk his claws deeper into the bark.

"Maybe you could bend the tree far enough over so's I kin reach him," said the missus.

Billy Bob put 'er in granma and bore down. He bent the tree nearly double. Missus was bouncin' on her toes desperately tryin' to grab the cat when the rope broke!

The last time they saw the cat he was goin' out over the top of the house like a furry mortar shell.

Half a mile away, Bubba and his sweet lil' daughter, Wava Dean, were havin' a grape NeHi out by the pool behind their ranch house.

"Wava Dean, I'm tellin' ya fer the last time, you can't have a cat. They git hair all over everything, harass the chickens and never say thank you. Now don't ask me again!"

As Wava Dean wiped a tear from her pretty eye, out of the clear blue of the western sky, like a space capsule re-entering the atmosphere, came that dang cat! He made a perfect four-point splash down in the middle of the pool!

Bubba looked up. There wuddn't a cloud in the sky.

"Wava Dean, sugar, will you look at that! Yer prayers have been answered!"

COSTA COUNTY, CALIFORNIA PR 6 & 175

COUNTY ORDINANCE

BE IT ENACTED BY LAW THAT

1) NO DOG OR ANY OTHER ANIMAL SHALL BE TRANSPORTED UNLESS TOTALLY ENCLOSED WITHIN THE VEHICLE OR SECURELY CROSS TETHERED.

MOVE OVER MA

Whoa back, boys! They are treading on sacred ground. Obviously it won't affect the man goin' to town with a load of turkeys on his flatbed or hunters comin' down the mountain with a six-point buck strapped across the hood, but . . . they don't want ol' Bingo bouncin' upon the tack box or hangin' his head over the side.

The wording of the law includes all animals, but whoever heard of anyone pullin' up to the coffee shop with two penguins or a moose in the truck? You never hear a cowboy shout "Go git in the pickup!" to a barn cat. No. This law is aimed specifically at dogs. Not just dogs, either . . . cow dogs, in particular. Your dog. Legislation like this is sponsored by well-meaning animal rights groups. Dog safety is their primary concern.

However, is it in the dog's best interest? One of the joys of bein' a dog (or a kid, for that matter) is bein' able to leap in the back of the pickup and go with the boss. The satisfyin' feelin' of stickin' yer head into the wind, hangin' yer tongue out and goin' down the road, is usually the high point of a dog's day. They get to see new sights, do a little barkin' and view the world from a little higher vantage point.

I made it a point to interview several dogs concerning these new laws. The cowdogs were 100% against such legislation. They said, "How would you feel if the government made it a law that humans had to wear seat belts, crash helmets and drive under 55 mph!"

I interviewed two bird dogs who, between them had the IQ of a sandhill crane. They had very little to add.

But since dogs don't vote, none of their opinions carry much value. The solution, I guess, is to let yer dog ride in the front. Between the cardboard box of old syringes and the door. "Move over, Ma. You know Blue likes the window."

OL' BLUE

"I loved ol' Blue as much as a man
could love a man's best friend
An' when his time came I helped him along
I owed him that much in the end."

In the fall when I go out to preg check the cows the neighbors all show up to help. They come in about daylight each of 'em drivin' a big four-wheel drive pickup with stock racks on the back. They got a handy man jack and two spares tied to the side and in the back of each pickup is, at least one GOOD DOG . . . and two pups!

Now these dogs leap out an' commence to fight with one another for about two hours! You spend the rest of the day kickin'em out from under your feet or chasin'em outta the gate!

But you can't say nothin', oh, no! It's a sacred thing! You can't criticize another man's dog! So in self defense I wrote this little poem which I entitled, simply,

THE COWBOY AND HIS DOG

There's a scene that is really pictorial
That's been here since time immemorial
The cowboy out riding, his dog right beside him
Somehow it's almost historial.

They come in all colors and sizes
From dingos all full of surprises
Blue-eyed scene stealers and Queensland blue heelers
And collies that win lots of prizes.

He responds to your love and affection
And waits on his master's direction
You say, "Put'em in!", and watch with a grin
While he obeys your command to perfection.

And just when you start to go braggin'
On that cow eatin' wonder, you're draggin'
The dog you admire, will piss on a tire
Or go lick his nuts in the wagon!

There's nothin' that makes me mad quicker
Than a dog in the wrong baliwicker,
You can't find your niche, you son of a bitch!
Go git in the pickup, pot licker!

THE LOST DOG

Evenin' Joe . . .

I hope I didn't wake y'all, I know it's after nine
  But I got a little problem, so to speak.
I don't know how to tell this, I feel a little dumb
  'Cause the little dog I had run off last week.

Yea, that bouncin' blue eyed mongrel, you know the one I mean.
  He rides with me and sleeps on Mother's lap.
We got 'im when the kids left just a year or two ago
  And I reckon that he sorta fills a gap.

I was up on Saddle Mountain to scatter out some salt
  And he musta fell out when I started home.
I came out down by yer place and if he shows up there
  I'd appreciate a jingle on the phone.

He really isn't worth much but Ma got plum upset.
  Seems 'round the ranch he's made himself a star.
No, I'm not really worried, but the way she carried on
  I better find him, ya know how women are.

I've phoned all of the neighbors and backtracked to the camp
  And called for him until my throat is sore.
And I really wouldn't bother but I like the little cuss . . .
  Just a minute, Joe, there's someone at the door.

Hello, Joe. You'll never guess! Ma, come take a look at this!
  He's back! Say, Joe, I'll see you at the brandin'.
You crazy little buggar, come sit in Daddy's lap . . .
  See ya, Joe. And Joe, thanks for understandin'.

THE REST OF US

He used to break horses, he used to herd sheep,
He worked in a feedlot a while.
He grew up a'dreamin' he'd buy him a ranch
And raise horses and cattle in style.

But time pulled a fast one, life took a turn,
Dreams pulled the wool o'er his eyes,
'Cause it takes more than wishin' and workin' all day
To buy you a ranch and survive.

So now he sells saddles, or vaccine, or seed,
Or writes for the Livestock Gazette,
Doin' whatever it takes to stay close
To the land that he'll never get.

In ag economics or ranch real estate,
In his hat and his boots and his gloves,
Collectin' his check as he goes down the road
From the folks that he wishes he was.

Hell, he knows he's lucky to just have a job
That lets him stay close to his roots.
He may never own the ranch of his dreams
But at least he can pay for his boots.

LIVIN' IN TOWN

Livin' in town, boys, is hard, Lord, it's hard
Why, even the dog don't like the backyard.

I've spent all my life on the back of a horse
And that is a life I'd be glad to endorse

'Cept I've got a new baby, a kid startin' school
And it's tough to pay bills ridin' colts, packin' mules.

And so we gave notice and moved into town
But it's just for a while, 'til we get the down

To buy us a place to run a few cows
And a horse for the kid 'cause she ain't got one now.

A place where my wife can look up at the stars
Hear crickets and coyotes, not a chorus of cars

And I can go out in the cool evenin' air
And pee off the porch with no neighbors to care.

Maybe I'm dreamin', but dreamin's okay
They help an ol' cowboy to git through the day.

So I set on the couch after they've gone to bed
And hear the refrig as it hums in my head

And stare at the street light as sirens go by
Rememberin' when we came here and why.

I give my ol' brain some time to unwind
Knowin' tomorrow it's back to the grind.

I'll pet my ol' dog 'fore I turn out the light
He's wishin', like me, we wuz elsewhere tonight.

But for the time bein' our dreams have to wait
'Cause reality comes in the mornin' at eight.

COFFEE SHOP COMMUNION

You'll find 'em at the sale barn
They've got the front row seat
But they ain't bought a day-old calf
Since Gerald Ford got beat.

They gather at a farm sale
Although they never bid
They'll tell you if you paid too much
And, sure enough . . . you did!

They cover all the bases,
Like doctors makin' rounds,
To get each gruesome detail right
And then they meet in town.

At coffee shop communion
Where reg'lar clientele
Present their unique points of view
Like it was show and tell.

They sift through all the gossip
Like judges on the bench
And search to find a shred of truth
Among the evidence.

What's happened to the country?
What's wrong with kids today?
Who was the last good Democrat?
How 'bout the price of hay?

They solve the world's problems,
Sacrificing to it,
And if you ask 'em, Why?, they say,
"Someone's gotta do it."

Lord knows it isn't easy
When mankind's gone awry
But still they toil, pausing just
To take a bit of pie.

They've raised their humble pastime
To greatness, there's no doubt
And they deserve a black belt in
The art of hangin' out.

A shrine should be erected
In every town's cafe
In honor of the miracles
Performed there without pay.

"Upon this site each weekday,"
Would read the simple plaque,
"Six deacons in their seed corn caps
Turn rumors into fact!"

BANK of
AROUND THE WORLD BARBER SHOP
MAGGIE'S TOWN CAFE
BOB BLACK

LIFE BEYOND FORTRAN

There's a certain group of people that circulate in and out of the cattle business like smoke in Peb & Fergie's Bar. They're the accountants, bookkeepers, bankers and programmers. Often unappreciated, they worship at the feet of a strange guru; the computer. This poem's for them.

There's a natural resentment
When we don't understand,
For technical advances
Attributed to man.

Now I'm learning evolution
And positions of the stars
And why it is, that wives, most times,
Don't like you in the bars.

But the greatest of inventions
That I have ever seen
Is the flashing phosphorescence
Of a C.R.T.V. screen

For those of you unknowing,
It's part of a computer
That makes us all seem wise somehow,
Smarter and astuter.

But I guess the thing that chaps me
Is it never makes mistakes!
It's always human error,
Power surges, earthquakes!

It's what you put into it
That determines your reward.
Like dealin' square with strangers
And givin' part back to the Lord.

Commandment number seventeen
Is what it's all about;
Computin's just like livin'
Garbage in and garbage out!

YOUR OUT'A BUSINESS
-10,000
-13,000
BILLS

COLDER THAN A BANKER'S HANDSHAKE

Jake, it's time for a chat. I'm just reviewing your loan.
I would have come over or give you a call
But they told me you took out your phone!

Remember the audit in '80? Your books were a flippin' disgrace!
I lent you enough for an adding machine
But you bought a new horse in its place!

And the flood of '75. You said it was good for the grass.
Jake's Frog and Fish Farm; I extended the note.
You went in hock clear up to your bass!

I financed your crazy ideas; the turkeys, the comfrey and more
The Christmas tree venture, the miracle fence
And the tourist trap with the dinosaur!

I wrote off the gold mine and the trained buffalo.
When you went into Amway I bought all your soap!
Then absorbed the loss on your Wild West Show.

I've stuck by you, Jake, through thick and through thin
On each crazy notion that came in your head
But this latest request is the end!

I can't take the risk. It can't be allowed.
How do you think a bank can break even
Makin' a loan on a set of ol' cows!

LOANS
AWARD
Be it known that this particular loan officer is one shrewd cookie
7/4/14 El Bosso
JAKE'S WILD WEST SHOW
Jake's MIRACLE FENCE
APPLICATION
ANOTHER APPLICATION
JAKE
Yet another application
BOB BLACK

JEKYLL & HIDE CATTLE COMPANY

He's kind to his wife when the market goes up
His children think that he's neat.
The implement dealer sits by him in church
And his banker waves on the street.

Salesmen treat him like he was a king
The hired man asks for a raise.
The press is reporting exorbitant gains
But P.C.A.'s singin' his praise!

A genius, he humbly admits to himself,
Smart as a tree full of owls!
Twenty foot tall with a bullet proof brain
And a friend to all of his pals!

But something occurs when the market goes down.
His family feels it first.
The mother-in-law gives him plenty of room
And the dog gets reg'larly cursed!

He gets lots of mail from lawyers in town.
The gas man won't fill up the tank.
The feed company rep has forgotten his name!
He's a leper down at the bank!

His ulcer is worse. His accountant's in jail!
They repo'd the pickup he had.
His levi's don't fit. They bag in the rear
They've chewed on his tail so bad!

He might get discouraged, but down at the sale
His heart will rejuvenate.
A gambler in spirit whose living depends
On the fickle finger of fate!

So just like the story of Jekyll and Hyde
He's a wise man or a clown.
A hero or fool depending on whether
The market goes up . . . or goes down!

FEED
CLOSED
FEED

DUTY

It's hard to be a penguin when yer heart's a sandhill crane.
When yer more at home a'horseback than flyin' on a plane.
When peaceful country evenin's mean more than city lights
And clear blue skies outweigh the lure of fancy banquet nights.

Last year at the meeting you made me president.
The time's gone by so quickly I'm not sure where it went.
It surely was an honor and I did the best I could
But to tell the truth, my friends, my speakin's not that good.

I'm better on a tractor, countin' cows or pullin' shoes
But I'll say without a stutter I believe in what we do.
Our opinions are important, I feel it in my heart
So I'll stand up and take my turn, I'm glad to do my part.

I've talked to politicians and lobbied for our rights,
Spent hours on the telephone, spent many sleepless nights,
Then left the farm too often to my family and my wife,
And tried to represent us all, our problems and our life.

Sometimes I was successful. Sometimes you pulled your hair.
A man can be no better than the folks who put him there.
You overlooked my stumbling, even more than I deserve,
But what makes me the proudest . . . I had the chance to serve.

REP
BOB BLACK

GRADUATION

"I'll make you proud you sent me," said the boy to his dad
As the two of them reviewed his senior year.
"Sis became a dentist, and I know it made you glad
That Johnny Boy's a civil engineer.

Both your brothers came and lived with us a while
Before they went to study at State U.
Plus Mama's little sister who became a licensed nurse,
I know you sent her some to help her through.

Sis has built a clinic that's the envy of the town.
I reckon it was you co-signed her note.
Uncle Bob and Uncle Bill were thankful for that loan
You made to keep their businesses afloat.

We kept Aunt Kathryn's children at the time of her divorce
'Til she got work and got back on her feet.
I guess that I'm the last one, Dad, to leave the feathered nest
And, by the way, this new car's really neat.

Dad, I've often wondered, does it ever bother you
That all your family's educated right,
While you, yourself, quit grade school and went to work at home,
Does that fact ever keep you up at night?"

"Well, son, I guess I'd always hoped to do more with my life
But I'm thankful for the chances I was given.
All this time while you been learnin', you been earnin' a degree
And I was only earnin' us a livin'."

BOB BLACK

THE AG SURVIVAL TEST

Will you be able to survive in agriculture? Here is a test designed to help you evaluate your chances. Your answers will determine whether you are financially and psychologically fit to continue. Please circle either A) or B).

1. My present financial portfolio includes:
   A) over one million in land and livestock free and clear
   B) a ten year old Ford ¾ ton, 6 horses worth 32 cents a pound and a wife with a job.
2. Most of my ready cash is in:
   A) interest bearing checking accounts
   B) a Copenhagen lid on the bedroom dresser.
3. My banker calls me:
   A) "Mister"
   B) every two hours
4. My idea of a sound financial investment is:
   A) undeveloped pasture in downtown Dallas
   B) a racing greyhound
5. My chances of getting a loan are:
   A) sure as the sun rises
   B) as good as Slim Whitman becoming Pope (Pope Slim I)
6. The best cattle deal I ever made was:
   A) sold 3,000 head of 28 cent Corrientes for 56 cents three months later
   B) stole a truckload of feeder calves and lost $30 a head
7. I started ranching because:
   A) I love the land and inherited $5 million
   B) my daddy chained me to a tractor when I was 6 years old
8. My long term economic plans include:
   A) expansion and increased productivity
   B) winning the jackpot team roping next Friday
9. I intend to ranch and farm as long as I can:
   A) make money
   B) borrow money
10. The reason I ranch and farm today is:
    A) I find it a fascinating and lucrative profession
    B) I'm in too deep to quit

RESULTS: If you circled all A's, you are an optimistic management type with oil on your property. It is highly likely you will survive and invest in satellite technology.

If you circled all B's, you are presently engaged in modern marginal agricultural practices. You will be here tomorrow and the next day, and the next, and the next. Because somebody will always have to be there to do the work.

HIC
HIC
OLD CROW
SHARP DECLINE IN FEEDER PRICES

HANGIN' ON, HOPIN' AND PRAYIN' FOR RAIN

There's a fingernail moon hangin' low in the sky.
The crickets make small talk as he passes by.

As the gentlest breeze stirs what's left of his hair
He spits and he sniffs it, but no moisture there.

He stares at the field and remembers the year
These same eighty acres paid the loan free and clear.

But these last thirty days have scared him to death.
The dirt's as dry as a horny toad's breath.

He called up his banker after supper tonight,
They talked for an hour and he's sure gettin' tight.

Ol' Thelma had kissed him and went on to bed
So he took a walk, thought it might clear his head.

The doctor has told him he has to slow down,
Sell out the home place and move into town.

'Move into town! What the hell would he do?'
He shook off the thought and took a fresh chew.

A bachelor cloud, thin as fog on a mirror,
Crossed over the moon and then disappeared.

He sniffs at the air that's still dry as a bone,
And takes one more look at the seeds that he's sown.

He'll be back tomorrow if somethin' don't change,
Just hangin' on, hopin', and prayin' for rain.

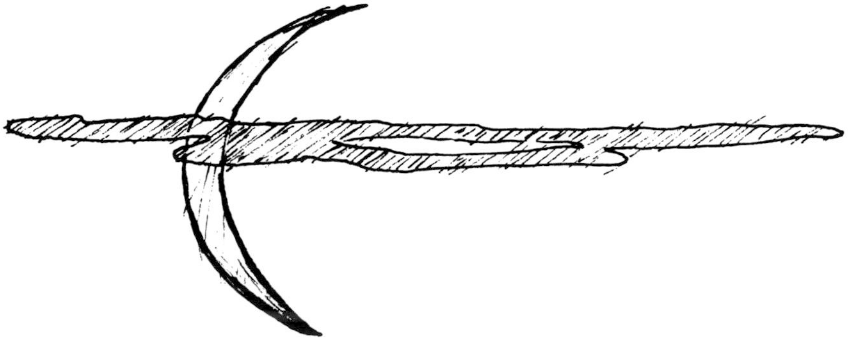

BOB
BLACK

TAKE CARE OF YER FRIENDS

Friend is a word that I don't throw around
Though it's used and abused, I still like the sound.
I save it for people who've done right by me
And I know I can count on if ever need be.

Some of my friends drive big limousines
Own ranches and banks and visit with queens.
And some of my friends are up to their neck
In overdue notes and can't write a check.

They're singers or ropers or writers of prose
And others, God bless'em, can't blow their own nose!
I guess bein' friends don't have nothin' to do
With talent or money or knowin' who's who.

It's a comf'terbul feelin' when you don't have to care
'Bout choosin' your words or bein' quite fair
'Cause friends'll just listen and let go on by
Those words you don't mean and not bat an eye.

It makes a friend happy to see your success.
They're proud of yer good side and forgive all the rest
And that ain't so easy, all of the time
Sometimes I get crazy and seem to go blind!

Yer friends just might have to take you on home
Or remind you sometime that you're not alone.
Or ever so gently pull you back to the ground
When you think you can fly with no one around.

A hug or a shake, whichever seems right
Is the high point of givin', I'll tellya tonight,
All worldly riches and tributes of men
Can't hold a candle to the worth of a friend.

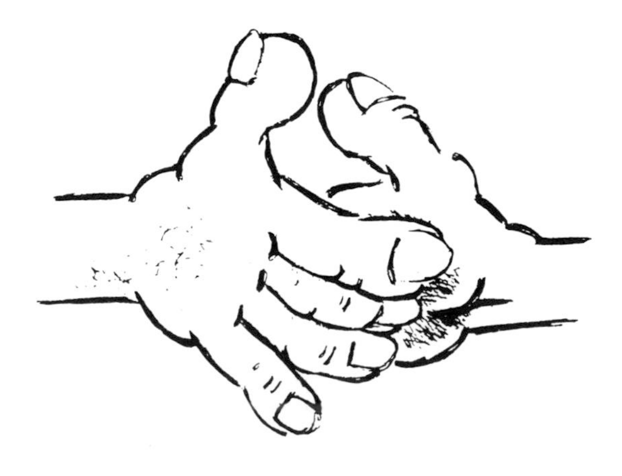

AIRPORT
ENTRANCE
PEACE & LOVE THE MOONIES
1982 ©

SOME COWBOY PHILOSOPHY

Quotations gathered from cowboy friends and people I admire.

"Indian build little fire. White man build big fire.
White man get warm carrying wood."

On the subject of fire building, "A good Indian always
carries a can of gas."

"If two fellas never argue it jus' means one of 'em's
doin' all the thinkin'."

"Everyday is Saturday to a dog."

"Country people don't shine their shoes very often;
but they don't shine other people's either."

On killin' time, "Just circlin' like a man with one oar."

"I can't understand it; they built a brand new jail
in the county seat and then filled it with riff raff!"

"Milkin' a thousand cows is like havin' a thousand wives."

"In a card game you go by the golden rule; him who
has the gold makes the rules."

"Tourists come to Owyhee county with a pair of cutoff jeans and a
twenty dollar bill and don't change either one 'til they leave!"

"A cowboy and his money are soon parted."

"Never assume nothin'; there's two things a cowboy don't know
anything about; one of 'em's a cow and the other's a horse!"

PEOPLE ARE FUNNY CRITTERS

There's

Apple pie bakers and crooked bookmakers
Blondes and brunetters and birthday forgetters
Chicken fry lovers and blue-eyed soul brothers
Drinkers and boozers and winners and losers
Elephant trainers and tireless campaigners
Fixers and menders and paper clip benders
Goers and stayers and pinochle players
Handkerchief users and tissue abusers
Interstate bikers and wilderness hikers
Joggers and addicts and handball fanatics
Kissers and tellers and friends of the fellers
Lovers and fighters and fingernail biters
Mayonnaise dippers and Miracle Whippers
Newspaper readers and drivers and speeders
Overweight hookers and magazine lookers
People with answers and bottomless dancers
Quivering flunkers and basketball dunkers
Readers and thinkers and double scotch drinkers
Soda straw manglers and bar napkin stranglers
Teasers and cryers and high rollin' fliers
Uncles and sisters and passive resisters
Virtuous girlies and sillies and squirrelies
Weirdos and sickies and five dollar quickies
Xylophone pickers and popsicle lickers
Yawners and nappers and one handicappers
Zippy old timers and lunatic rhymers . . .

people are funny critters

WELCOmE PARADE
ROD
FANS
JOES
WILD
RODE
EVER
COORS
BEER
VOTE
1980

PEOPLE ARE FUNNY CRITTERS CHAPTER TWO

There's

Artichoke peelers and ex-Pittsburgh Steelers
Building erectors and true genuflectors
Chewbacca rooters and hard eight crap shooters
Down in the dumpsters, measlers and mumpsters
Electrical wizards with spark in their gizzards
Flakey fast talkers and wild turkey stalkers
Garbanzo bean eaters and chronic repeaters
Happy go luckers, goosers and duckers
Illusive bill payers, watchers and players
Jugglers and punters and cardiac shunters
Krackle Korn crunchers and martini lunchers
Lookingbill spotters and 3-gaited trotters
Mare ridin' mothers and ol' Tommy Smothers
Nuisance creators and foul catfish baiters
Oliver Twisters and squabblin' sisters
Pulitzer writers and persimmon biters
Quacky ol' doctors and potion concoctors
Right handed wipers, plumbers and pipers
Silver tongued devils and men on the level
Tit clingin' babies and wine drinkin' maybes
Unfulfilled maidens with hearts heavy laden
Vocal exclaimers and name droppin' namers
Wild parachuters and 5-buckle booters
X rated peekers and Kiowa Creekers
Yacht racin' crazies and barn sour lazies
Zany 'don't throw its!' and maniac poets

people are funny critters

Coors
HIC
HIC
pittsburgh
STEELER
8
©1982

LUTHER AND THE DUCK HUNTIN'

Well, lemme tell ya 'bout my cousin, Luther. Now Luther married Uncle Dink's little girl, Amelda. They lived in Plainview a while, then they moved to Ft. Worth where he works for the paper.

Them people down in Oklahoma an' Texas, boy, they are hunters! An' Luther is one jus' like'm. He is a hunter's hunter! Hunt and fish; avid!

He called one winter an' said he wanted to come up and visit an' I said, "Gosh, Luther, be glad to have ya!" Which I wuz.

When they showed up they hadn't been here five minutes when he said he'd shore like to go huntin.' Now I don't hunt much myself. Don't mean anything by it, jus' don't care for it one way or t'other. But Luther wanted to go huntin'. He'd heard all about my home state and read our advertizin' in the Sports Afield. 'Bout how we had all kinds of birds, big game an' good fishin' and everything else.

I said, "Luther, it's the middle of the winter!"

"Oh," he said, "There's gotta be somethin' open. Call the Fish and Game!"

So I did an' shornuf, it wuz DUCK SEASON!

Now I don't mind tellin' ya, if a guy's gotta nice camper, and a good place to park it an' he can walk from there to the edge of the lake without gettin' his feet wet, ya know, I don't mind huntin'. But I got to tell you, there are some crazy people in the world and the craziest of all them people is duck hunters!

Lay out there in the middle of the winter in that freezin' weather in water clear up to their buckle an' then shoot a duck! I jus' never developed a taste for it, I guess.

But Luther had to go! So we went out an' hunted all day out on the edge of the lake amongst the cattle. Didn't get duck number one!

We come in that night an' I wuz frozen solid! But Luther said, "I tell ya what. There's plenty o' ducks out there, we jus' ain't gettin' close enough."

I said, "What are we gonna do?"

He said, "I gotta idea. We'll disguise ourselves as a cow. Then we can sneak right up on 'em."

I said, "Are you crazy! Where are we gonna git a cow disguise!"

He said, "Call the packin' house."

So we go down to Armour and picked one up. A big old soggy wet hide with the head still on it. It weighed two hundred pounds! Real fresh. Had big horns.

So there we are the next morning. The sun comin' up over the lake. We're walkin' along the edge of the bank there. Luther's in the front, holdin' up the head and peerin' out through the eye holes. I'm hikin' along there in the back peekin' out . . .

When all of a sudden I see somethin'! I grab Luther by the leg, I say, "Luther! Look around here, boy!"

Luther, he look around an' comin' up behind us wuz a GREAT BIG BULL. I mean that sucker had a smile on his face an' he wuz comin' our way!!!

I said, "Luther! Whatter we gonna do?"

He said, "I'm gonna start grazin', you better brace yerself!"

SALMON FISHING

So you might say to yerself, "What does a boy raised on the New Mexico desert know about salmon?" Well, before I went to Ilwaco, WA, all I knew was that you could buy fluorescent salmon eggs to fish for trout. But we called 'em Patooshki Fireballs.

The Columbia River reaches a boil about the time it dumps into the Pacific Ocean. I went with a bunch of cowboy types on a salmon fishing trip. We gathered the night before and proceeded to celebrate, cowboy style.

Morning came before the sun rose. Our sadistic guide and captain insisted we eat a big meal before embarking. At 4 a.m. I entered the bustling restaurant and optimistically ordered the "Fisherman's Special." It was biscuits and gravy, corned beef hash, three eggs, hash browns, toast and jelly, short stack, ham, sausage, bacon, orange juice and coffee. Confidently I boarded the Leprechaun.

In the gray light of dawn we sailed for the bar. Not the one from the night before, this bar was a mile long rock wall that kept the Pacific from washin' away Oregon! The captain commented in passing that we were now over the biggest ship graveyard on the continent. Rounding the bar, waves dwarfed our 38-foot fishing boat.

I sat down in the cabin with the troops for a few minutes as the boat peaked and dove like a pingpong ball in a Cuisinart. I hiccuped. It tasted like corned beef hash. The diesel fumes were makin' me nauseous. I stepped out on the after deck for some fresh air. I was promptly submerged by a crashing wave. Returning to the confined cabin I sat while my stomach kept trying to stand. Donning my slicker, I went back up on deck.

By the time we reached the fishing spot, my face looked like two pearl onions in a creme de menthe. The engines stopped but the boat kept rocking. I unceremoniously scattered my "Fisherman's Special" over the leeward side.

The after deck had a bait box, about the size of a casket right in the center. Twelve people lined up around it and fished over the sides and back. The head (ask your Navy friends) was level with the deck beside the entrance to the cabin.

I lay for hours on the deck beside the bait box in the agony of seasickness that only fellow sufferers can appreciate. With the last of my strength, I staggered to the head to gag in private and pray for a Coast Guard helicopter. I clutched my stomach and realized I was also afflicted by that most undignified and unwelcome of maladies, yes, friends, I was hit by the demon, Scours!

Maneuvering in the cramped head, I reversed positions just as the boat was rocked by a tidal wave. The door slid open and I shot out on deck! Pants around my knees, off balance, out of breath and embarrassed.

I careened around the bait box, bouncing back and forth on the slippery, seesawing deck like a pickled beet in a pin ball machine. I was takin' little bitty steps! I completely circumnavigated the bait box and crashed back in the head where I remained, and am, to this day.

JACK RABBIT
POTATOS
BOB BLACK

MY LAST WILL AND SEDIMENT

Bein' of sound mind and body
Though lackin' a full set of brains,
I been rackin' and snackin' and double back trackin'
On how to bequeath my remains.

I don't take this duty too lightly
Though most would ask themselves why?
What possible use would this sorry excuse
Of a body be worth when I die?

My liver, I'm sure would be useful
For holdin' down tarps on the hay,
Settin' up traps or weight water gaps
Or fillin' a land fill someday.

My foot could be used as a ruler.
My hand could be lent to a friend.
For a rickety table my leg would be able
To make it be stable again.

My tongue could be hooked to the wagon.
My hair would make a toupee
To keep you from harm you could hold up my arm
To stay the right distance away.

You could use my nose on the grindstone.
My fingers are handy to read;
To end arguments, at sporting events
Or in traffic when you feel the need.

To further explain I've made up a list
Of parts to be used if you can.
There just might be others but sisters and brothers,
Remember, I'm only one man.

I'm available to:
keep an eye on the wife
pull a truck with my toe
nail a crook to the wall
belly up to a bar
bone up on your studies
leave my heart by the bay
put a shoulder to the wheel
hang out in sleazy joints
rope a calf, have a ball
take my breath away
spill my guts, take no lip
build an elbow room off the garage
thumb a ride, ear a horse down
put some teeth in a law
rib somebody, back up a pardner
or if you just need to get a head, call me.

On second thought;
Being of sound mind and body, I'm taking everything with me.

R.I.P.
BAB
DVM
HE HELPED MANY
A FAIR MAIDEN
THE
LAST WAS MARRIED
1982

HOT CROSS BUNS

Fred (an alias) was one of those fellers that attracted lightening. Storm clouds followed him like horn flies on a bull's back. He was always limping, squinting or groaning as the result of some injury. It became a source of personal embarrassment.

His family and friends constantly admonished him to "Be Careful!" but he was jinxed. Like the January when he decided to shovel a blizzard's accumulation of snow off his roof. In an effort worthy of O.S.H.A., he took his rope and made himself a safety line.

He secured one end to the back bumper of his pickup in the front yard. Looping the other end of the rope around his waist, he went up on the roof and over the peak. His wife left for town . . . in his pickup. Broke both his legs, his pelvis and one wrist.

During recovery he was sitting around the house in a cumbersome body cast. His wife had the habit of filling her cigarette lighter with fluid over the commode. Later that afternoon ol' Fred creaked his way into the bathroom like a NASA moonwalker. He maneuvered himself into position and lowered himself, cast and all, down on the seat. Exhausted, but smugly satisfied with his achievement, he lit a cigarette and dropped the match into the lurking lighter fluid. It blew him into the tub and broke his other wrist!

We're talkin' hot cross buns! If you ever wondered where the word "embarrass" came from . . .

Ford
BOB BLACK

FIXIN' THE OUTHOUSE

The ol' man wuz layin' there on the sofa and the ol' lady come in and said, "Git out there and fix that outhouse!"

The ol' man got up and ambled out and hammered a few nails in and come back in and laid down. Here she come!

"I thought I told you to git out there and fix that outhouse!" He snapped offa there a little quicker. He went out and hammered that piece of tin that had been flappin' all winter and he come back in and laid down. Here she come!

"You sorry ol' buzzard! If you don't get out there and fix that outhouse I'm gonna slap you into next week!"

He come offa there like a rocket! He run out to the shop and got his tools. He got his shovel and went around the foundation; hammered every nail in and set it! He took them little pieces of tar and patched that tin roof. He tightened that hinge up and greased'er, he went over that sucker with a fine tooth comb! She come out to see what wuz takin' him so long.

He was givin' it such a thorough inspection. He had his head down inside the hole, peerin' around . . .

She spooked him!

He jerked his head outta that hole and caught his chin whiskers in a crack in the lip of the seat right there!

"Dadgummit!" he said.

She said, "Aggrivatin', ain't it?"

TOMBSTONE OF CANAAN

WANTED: A cowpoke to help gather pairs
Dogs welcome, but not if they bark.
Non-drinker preferred, to help with the herd,
Signed, Noah, the U.S.S. Ark.

Now Tombstone of Canaan was broke
And, of late, had been offa the sauce,
So he rode to the yacht, was hired on the spot
And became Noah's buckaroo boss.

"Get two of each creature on Earth."
His orders were clear and precise.
To which he replied, "Does that include flies?
And roaches and woolies and mice?"

He set out like he was possessed,
He roped and delivered two skunk.
Two pigs in a poke, an egg, double yolk,
Two elephants stuffed in their trunk.

Two jack eye, a double entendre,
Two fish sticks still stuck to the pan
Giraffes, neck and neck, he led to the deck
But oysters he left in the can.

He tried to get two of each specie
A male and his counterpart
But tied in the willows were twelve armadillos
'Cause he couldn't tell 'em apart.

He rode to the mountain and looked in the woods
He even went downtown a'chasin'
Did the best that he could, brought 'em back on the hood,
Two elk, two moose and a mason.

This work had mellowed ol' Tombstone
His heart became tender and supple.
Recanting his vow, he let in a cow
And even a Methodist couple.

Then Noah took Tombstone aside,
"I'd hire you for forty more days
If I could be sure, you'd avoid the lure
Of the driftin' cowboy ways.

But I'm leery of takin' a cowboy.
They just up and leave on a whim.
And though I've resisted, my arm could be twisted
If I knew that you couldn't swim!"

The horse, a distinctive and special specie of animal, each individual of which has a personality and appearance all his own and this poem is dedicated to those people, who go by many names, who can look at a day old colt one time . . . and pick that sucker outta the string twelve years later.

THE HORSE

If the subject is horses, I'll say
I work with'em day after day
Big ones and small ones
Short ones and tall ones
From black ones to ol' dapple grays.

And in makin' my rounds I observe
The creatures I studied to serve
Some are polite
Some offer to bite
And some of 'em tested my nerve.

But I tried to make friends with 'em all
So they'd remember when I come to call
Each one is unique
Whether mighty or meek
In pasture or paddock or stall.

And when they say he's a son once removed
And show me the papers to prove
I nod and agree
'Cause I want'em to see
That the bloodline is one I approve.

And I smile when they point to that chart
And remark that the horse is right smart
But they'd not be impressed
If they knew I confessed
That I can't tell the buggars apart!

TRADIN' HORSES

Horse traders are an uncommon lot. Matter of fact, to be a good horse trader you have to be born with the ability. It's a congenital defect. Sort of a cross between a Ginzu steak knife salesman and a pickpocket.

They have the cunning of a coyote, the shrewdness of an order buyer, the memory of an IRS computer and the conscience of a flat rock.

They place very little value on fancy horse barns, matching truck and trailers, white fences, expensive saddles or two party checks. They get no thrill from owning a good horse. They're only good for one thing . . . to trade. The thrill is in the deal.

Uncle Albert was a horse trader. He never had a good horse. If he did, he never had it for long. He'd sell it. He always maintained a used horse lot. And like any smooth operator, he had just what you needed. He could make the lame walk (for a couple hours), the bad actors tame ('til the tranquilizer wore off), and the old, young again. "You want papers? It'll take a week. You want a palamino? Come back tomorrow."

Uncle Albert never did it for the money. He did it for the fun. For the pure simple joy of wheelin' and dealin'. Now before you get the idea Uncle Albert was unethical, you should understand the rules of horse tradin' . . . there aren't any! May the best man win and the other git skinned!

On the roundup Uncle Albert always furnished the wagon. It carried everybody's bed roll, war bag, brandin' irons, flour, canned goods, pots, pans, hammer, nails and extra gear. Of course, he also furnished the team that pulled the wagon. Each year it was a different team of horses. Green broke, sour, kickin', spooky typical trader renegades.

I noticed Uncle Albert pulled the tarp down real tight over the wagon and tied it down with about ten miles of rope. He went back and forth, over the top, around the tongue and under the wagon with the rope 'til it looked like the tangled line on King Kong's fishin' reel.

The new buckaroo said, "Ol' man, whatta ya think yer doin? Yer usin' way too much rope."

Uncle Albert said, "Nope, sonny. Every year these new hosses manage to turn the wagon over two or three times before I get'em gentled proper. An' this is a whole lot easier than pickin' everything up!"

FLOUR
XXX

THE HORSE TRADER

Have I got a deal for you. Got this horse on a trade.
He don't squint half as bad ridin' him in the shade.

I know he limps a little. Yer eyeball is astute.
But fair is fair, my friend, so I'll throw in a case of Bute.

No! He ain't got the heaves! Though I know he looks the part.
He's just a heavy breather, but he's got a lot of heart.

Bloodlines? Talkin' royal blue. A genuine contender.
I'll have these papers printed; fit any race you enter.

The would-be buyer of this horse just stared and shook his head.
He looked the trainer in the eye and said it when he said,

The only people that I know who'd ride *that* horse, I'd vow
Are too poor to ride a quarter horse n' too proud to ride a cow!

Honest Bob's Horses, Mules, & Bramer Bulls
366-7778
BUD

WHERE'S THE HORSE MEAT!

The horse has distinguished itself in the past
Through history in legend and song
While the cow has remained in the background
And I'll never argue it's wrong.
But what if their roles were inverted?
Then things would be different now.
We'd be dining on Thoroughbred T-bone
And Roy'd have ridden a cow.

Look back in time, had we eaten horses
The cow might have filled in the gaps.
Why, St. George would have needed a Holstein
To carry his pig-iron chaps.
We'd remember the great Trojan Guernsey
That slipped into town with a pull
And Atilla the Hun would have conquered
Astride of his polled Hereford bull.

Young buckaroos in the Jersey Express
Had vowed to deliver the mail.
Napoleon claimed a war might be lost
For want of a two gallon pail.
Imagine the great General Custer
As he speaks to his calvary line,
"Okay, Sergeant, have'm dismount,
Then unsaddle, it's milkin' time."

You could buy yer fast food at the race track.
The winner, no doubt, would be served.
The cafe'd be called the Red Gelding,
You can guess where they got the hors d'oeuvres.
Burritos would take on a new meaning,
The menu'd be Clydesdale filet,
The quarter pounder'd be old Quarter horse,
Dessert would be Shetland flammbe'.

Well, I guess Mr. Ed can be thankful
This poem's just my fancy ad libs,
'Cause Black Beauty would'a been Angus
And Trigger'd be barbecued ribs.
But I must have been dreamin' last weekend
At a horse show, where I stood aghast.
While the best Appaloosa they'd entered that day
Came in first — in the carcass class!

US
BOB BLACK

TO THE FEEDLOT HOSS

Boys, I offer a toast
To that creature tied to the post
Who through all his ills and occasional spills
Still gives us more than his most

He's black, bay or he's brown
Sorrel or spotted around
He eats that ol' hay even cows throw away
And makes his bed on the ground

'Round machinery and pumps that paddle
And trucks and gates that rattle
By a mill that roars he does his chores
He come here to jis' punch cattle

See them four brands on his side
The ones that wuz burnt in his hide
He's been around and covered more ground
Than we'd ever care to ride

For beauty he's often hard put.
Covered with mill dust and soot
But in a slick pen or a mud and snow blend
He'll go where you won't go afoot

In dust so thick you can't see
He breathes the same air that you breathe
And in a cold rain he feels that same pain
That numbs and stiffens yer knees

When the sun's beatin' down on yer head
And the rest of the day lies ahead
He's dreamin' too of the ranch he once knew
Where green grass and shade made a bed

Yup, he makes every step that you take
And feels each ache that you ache
And sweats, two fer one, every drop that you run
And seldom asks for a break

So before we mount up and start
Think twice of yer four-legged pard.
When he seems short on brains jus' give him the reins
'Cause boys, he's damn long on heart

HE WAS OK YESTERDAY...THEN BINGO!

"Doc, I called you just as soon
as I seen ol' Buck was sick.
He's been a little poorly
But he never missed a lick.

Last winter he got picky
And wouldn't eat his grain
So I gave him Doctor Bell's;
Tied garlic in his mane.

Then several months ago
When he started losin' weight
I give him Copenhagen
And a pound of catfish bait.

He come down with the splatters
And all his hair fell out!
So I fed him Larramycin
And Mother's sauerkraut.

Then last week after ridin'
He got as stiff as pine!
His navel needed smokin'
So I used the turpentine.

He went plum down on Sunday.
His kidneys, so I guessed.
I doctored up his water
And tied him facing west.

Last night I got to thinking'.
You were here two years ago.
You gave him some concoction
For a cough and runny nose.

I wondered if your treatment,
Which then improved his luck,
Had later turned against him
And poisoned my ol' Buck?

Whattya think, Doc?"

"DOC, WHILE YER HERE"...

Doc, sorry I called so late but you must be all through eatin'
I appreciate you comin' out. Yer truck shore took a beatin'
On my gravel road but I swear I'll get it graded.
I know I promised last time, but all this mud delayed it.

The cow's up in the pasture. I should'a called you sooner
But after lunch I took a nap, what Mama calls a nooner.
I read the mail and fed the dog and sat around and thought
Then I watched ONE LIFE TO LIVE, and Doc, I plum forgot.

Sorry 'bout this busted chute. I tried to get a welder.
But last time I used baler twine and I'm pretty sure it held'er.
I'm glad you brought a flashlight. This bulb's been out since May.
I'll have it fixed the next time I call you out this way.

Water? You mean drinkin' water? There's some in that old barrel.
But a rat drowned in there Tuesday so I'd be a little careful.
Oh, I just remembered, the kid's ol' Shetland pony
Got in a sack of barley and now he's actin' groany.

And since yer here already, the dog ain't had his shots.
The hogs' got diarrhea and I've been seein' spots.
If it's not too much to ask, would you use these pills I bought.
They're cheaper at the Co-op, Doc, you charge more than you ought.

I thank y'all fer comin', Doc, you've treated me alright.
I told the wife to call you first, especially late at night.
If you ever need a reference, I'll put you in my will
And about tonight's expenses . . . Just put it on my bill.

THE VET'S WIFE'S REFRIGERATOR

A scream from the kitchen. The thud of a faint.
She sighs and arises and walks with restraint.
Her neighbor lays peaceful, eyes fixed in a stare
She's passed out in front of the new Frigidaire.

She looks at the rack with eggs in its keep
Winking up at her's the eye of a sheep.
There's a bottle of PenStrep near the Swanson's pot pies
And down in the crisper's a bag full of flies.

The butter tray's filled with test tubes of blood
Marked, E.I.A. samples, from Tucker's old stud.
High on the shelf near a platter of cheese
Is a knotted, but leaking, obscene plastic sleeve.

Fecal containers are stacked, side by side,
With yesterday's pieces of chicken, home fried.
The freezer's a dither of guts, lungs and spleens
Scattered amongst the Birds Eye green beans.

Her home's a museum of animal parts.
Lymphomatous lymph nodes, selinium hearts.
Enough tissue samples to hold up a bridge
But why do they always end up in the fridge?

But she doesn't worry or turn up her nose,
She's the wife of a vet, it's the life that she chose.
But maybe he'd worry at lunch if he knew
He might just be dining on Whirl-Pack stew!

HOME BREW
Freezer
ICE MAKER
Swanson
Butter
Eggs
OYSTERS
ELASTRATIONS
BOB BLACK

THE SUPERSALESMAN

Slicker'n deer guts on a doorstep!
Smooth as a filly's nose!
Here in this jug's a miracle drug
So new that nobody knows!

Feed it, inject it or plant it,
Stick it under an ear.
Pick any breed, results guaranteed,
The data's perfectly clear.

It's good for foot rot in gophers,
Chafing on buffalo thighs,
Horses with corns, Angus with horns
And girls with fire in their eyes!

Goats with a bad disposition,
Lovers losing their spark,
Turpentined cats, blindfolded bats
And dogs that forgot how to bark!

Friends. Are you troubled with aphids?
Kids all down with the flu?
Cattle won't gain? Needing more rain?
I'll tellya what this'll do;

Kill all the weeds in your garden,
Patch up your innertube,
Leaven your bread, stiffen your thread
And work out your Rubik's cube!

Give you more miles per gallon,
Relieve your gastric distress,
If that ain't enough, this wonderful stuff
Eats barbecue stains off your dress!

I see you don't quite believe me!
The best I saved for last.
Pay me the cash then quick as a flash!
See? Oh, I went too fast.

Okay, let's do it again.
Watch and you'll understand.
Safe and improved, it gently removes
A five dollar bill from your hand!

GRRR
FEED
FARK!
FARK!
FARK!
OOF!
GROCERY LIST
DOCTOR BIMBOS GOOP $5
BOB BLACK

THE COYOTE

Take him for what he's worth, nothing more, nothing less.

I think I can speak for the coyote
With more understanding than most.
Especially those who defend him
And live on the New Jersey coast.

They raise up a pitiful cry
And claim he's a mistreated critter.
Who'll soon be extinct if the ranchers out west
Don't put down their rifles and quit'er.

But like all of God's creatures around us
There's always two sides to the tale.
I think if the coyote were human
That most of 'em would be in jail.

Cause there's no doubt he preys on the weaklings
Or the youngsters too little to run
He slits the throats of cute little lambs
And drags little calves from their mom.

So if you must describe him in terms
Such as wily, and clever and keen
You must also include homocidal,
Sadistic, demented and mean.

But I will choose to do neither
And somehow I wish you would, too.
For the coyote he has no conscience
He's just doin' the best he can do.

You can like and dislike the coyote,
Many ranchers I know do both
When he trespasses he'll get shot at
But his song in the night brings a toast.

A toast to our neighbor the coyote
Who'll outlive the earth and the sky.
And be here long after we've parted
Like the cockroach, the rat and the fly.

Several years ago we used to have some good people in the Bureau of Land Management but most of'em have got disgusted and left. Nowadays you gotta deal with the one-year wonders straight outta the suburbs who have been schooled in range management and come west with the lofty goal of protecting the environment from the evil rancher.

The latest addition to the harrassment is the E.I.S.; the Environmental Impact Statement. This huge document can be six inches thick and cost upwards of a million dollars!

E.I.S.

There's a predator stalking the plains
Who removes any reasonable doubt
That the government is bound and determined
To drive every cattleman out.

This affliction I'm talking about
To which the rancher's condemned
Is a shotgun wedding arrangement
To the government bride, B.L.M.

They thrive on words and confusion
And propagate each other like flies.
Each assistant's, assistant's, assistant
Has an assistant for him to advise!

All these people are needed
To create more work for themselves
And generate paper by truckloads
To keep busy the assistant elves.

If it's one thing they're dang good at
It's findin' projects to do.
Every insect and rodent and reptile
Is studied and counted for you.

If you want to know how many pellets
Of rabbit doo to the square mile
They've probably got volumes written
And stored in their warehouse on file!

The Environmental Impact Statement
The one they call E.I.S.
Is a bureaucrat's wish that's been granted
They can take more and leave you with less.

It allows them to ask for more money
And increase your grazing fee
Do more studies and write more papers
And hire more assistants, whoopie!

They're drowning themselves in assistants
In paperwork, pickups, and hell.
The only bad thing about it
Is they're drowning the rancher as well.

So, when they give me that E.I.S. notebook
As tall as a New York skyscraper,
I don't care how thick they make it
As long as it's on smooth paper!

E.I.S.
RABBIT
DROPING
REPORT

EAT AMERICAN LAMB

(50,000 COYOTES CAN'T BE WRONG)

The sheepman's got a problem now
Obtaining market price
Without offending everyone
Who wants his little slice.

The 'Back to Nature' advocates
In polyester smocks
Drink sacchrin tea in plastic cups
and curse the wooley flocks.

We've got a food stamp program,
TEN-EIGHTY'S bad, you see,
Now coyotes all have credit cards
And eat the lamb for free.

The A.U.M.'s are whittled down
To save us from ourselves.
Australia sends us mutton chops
To stock our grocer's shelves.

So pass the Vino Fino, boys
I'll offer up a plan
That will pull us all together
And meet each one's demands.

It will make the sheepman happy
Set coyotes minds at ease
The B.L.M., Sierra Club
And diplomats all pleased.

We can up our import quotas
Protect and be humane
By picking up Australian meat
In Forest Service planes.

Then scatter it from north to south
Near every herder's band
And let the coyotes on the range
Eat Australian lamb!

COOKED PRESSED MUTTON
NEW ZELAND LAMB CHOPS
DOWN UNDER LAMB

HELLO, I'M FROM THE GOVERNMENT...
I'M HERE TO HELP YOU

Mr. President, I guess we know you mean well
When you brag about the crops that we all raise
We can hold our heads up high when you talk of apple pie
And the prairies where our white face cattle graze.
When our beef cows finally started making money
You applied a price freeze for your next campaign
Then you lent us extra cash to plant wheat and succotash
Then slapped the old embargo on our grain.

There are programs to inspect each farmer's business
Be he milking cows or growing pinto beans
Our soil has been conserved and our wildlife is preserved
There's civil servants posting quarantines
We're required to fill out forms beyond all reason
From pesticides to predator control
From fertilizer use to the children we produce
The bureaucrats are always on patrol.

You tell us that we need your interference
Without your help you say we'd be a mess
We owe our lives to you, or, at least, you say we do
Not counting OSHA and the I.R.S.
But I think that we could feed us and our neighbors
With less help from your Washington machines
All we need is sun and rain, so I ask you, Don't complain
When your mouth is full of good ol' pork and beans.

The government should have three sacred duties
If Constitution guarantees prevail
To help us all survive; stay the hell out of our lives,
Protect our shores, deliver us the mail.
I appreciate the help that you've been giving
I'd even like to thank our Congressman
But please leave me alone, I can make it on my own
I've had all of your help that I can stand.

HATCHET RANCH
NECESSARY PERMITS
DOG BARKING #N3226
HORSE SADDLING #N3959
BREATHING #R1072
BEER DRINKING
BOOTS #T-532
SPIN
OUTLANDISH TAXES
MANDATORY JIVE
INCOMPREHENSIBLE VIOLATIONS
HAZARDOUS SAFETY REQUIREMENTS
HARASSMENT KIT # 146/J
RANCHERS AND FARMERS
DEPARTMENT OF INTERFERING BIMBOS
BOB BLACK

THE YOUNG POLITICIAN

He rose in the class, hand over his heart
And spoke of his future career
"The political ring's where I'll throw my hat
I love the applause and the cheers.

"I'll learn all the buzzwords, then make some up
Like mandate and flexible goals.
Ecoelastic alternative tax
With built-in confusing loopholes.

"Inflation, deflation, reliable source,
I'll climb the political rungs
And dazzle the voters with rhetorical quotes
And the art of speaking in tongues.

"I'll master the impasse and walk on the fence
I'll be brilliant, incisive and wise
When it comes time to put conscience aside
I'll vote for the best compromise."

He told all his friends 'bout running for 'pres'
The word got around in no time
His high school advisor took him aside
And laid all his doubts on the line.

"I doubt you'll ever be president, son"
He said, and I'm sure that he meant it,
"But with your attendance record so poor,
You might have a chance for the Senate!"

UNITED STATES
SENATE
I
ACCEPT
BOB
BLACK

FOOD IS FOR PEOPLE, NOT PROFIT!

You've heard it said, no doubt, by those
Who study social digs,
"The 3rd World sits a starvin'
While we feed corn to pigs."

To those of you who think like that
You've got some noble goals.
Yet, your altruistic logic
Contains some gaping holes.

See, someone has to pay the bill
To grow the grain you want.
'Cause if we outlawed feeding pigs
And sold to government

The only way that Uncle Sam
Could get repayed at all,
Is sell that grain to governments
With backs against the wall

Who probably can't afford it,
'Cause if they could, ya know,
They wouldn't be in trouble now,
They'd bought it long ago!

You're generous, which I admire,
To wish to give away
The fruits of farmers' labors
To those who cannot pay.

Then you and I and Farmer Brown
Would each be taxed our share
To send our bounty overseas
Until our cupboard's bare.

Then we'd achieve your noble goal;
Equality . . . but listen,
What good is equal poverty
Without a pot . . . to stand on?

ANIMAL LOVERS

Let's talk about animal lovers
Not those who protest and accuse
But everyday people who carry the load
And don't make the six o'clock news.

It's proper to make the distinction
When explanations are given;
Between those who care as a hobby
And others who care for a livin'.

When we speak of animal lovers
The part-time groups come to mind.
Nice enough folks, who articulate well,
And shine when the cameras grind.

It's too bad more credit's not given
To the ones who seldom get heard
'Cause, in spite of their modest behavior,
Their actions speak louder than words.

These are the folks that on Christmas Day
Take care of God's animals first
With never a thought they should have the day off
Or that they might be reimbursed.

They believe that Genesis meant it,
That man has dominion o'er all,
And they don't take their mandate too lightly
To care for the great and the small.

God's entrusted His creatures to us
By rating us all in His log
According to what our abilities are;
Most get a house cat or dog.

But the bulk of the animal kingdom
He placed in the hands of a few
Who feel more at home in a pasture than
An office on Fifth Avenue.

God did it that way for a reason
'Cause talk's cheap where carin's concerned.
The title of animal lover is
An honor that has to be earned.

To those who'd debate my conclusion
To your own you're welcome to cling.
But I'll bet if we'd ask His opinion
God knows that He did the right thing.

A CHRISTMAS TREE

A Christmas tree is one of those things
Like popcorn balls or angel wings
That children make in the snow

Things with beauty unsurpassed
That touch our lives but never last
More than a week or so

It shines from every living room
Like someone in a bright costume
That's happy to see you drop by

And in a world that never slows down
To see their lights all over town
Warms you up inside

And it's nice to get to know one well
To know each tinsel and jingle bell
That often as not don't ring

I can stare at the lights and never stop
Look back at the angel on the top
And imagine he can sing

Even the scraggliest Christmas tree
Seems to have some dignity
Guarding the gifts below

But all the ones I've seen up close
Seem to be smiling and acting the host
To all who say hello

Sometimes I think, if I were a tree
The most that I could hope to be
Is one of these wonderful pines

That gets to spend a week with friends
When even a grown-up kid pretends
That all the world is fine

Don Gill
1982 ©

ALL I WANT FOR CHRISTMAS

All my clothes are laundry
All my socks are fulla holes
I've got t.p. in my hatband
And cardboard in my soles.

I've stuffed the want ad section
Underneath my long-john shirt
And my jacket's held together
By dehornin' blood and dirt.

The leather on my bridle's
Been fixed so many times
My horse looks like that fence post
Where we hang the baler twine

When I bought that horse he was
As good as most around
But when I sold 'im last month
He brought thirteen cents a pound.

I've been unable lately
To invest in purebred cows
Since my ex-wives and their lawyers
Are dependents of mine, now.

See, my first wife took my saddle
The second skinned my hide
The third one got my deer head
And the last one took my pride.

I've had a run of bad luck
But I think it's gonna peak
'Cause my dog that used to bite me
Got run over just last week.

So all I want for Christmas
Is whatever you can leave
But I'd settle for a new wife
Who would stay through New Year's Eve.

December
SMTWTFS
WHEATIES
CRUNCHIES
12 12oz PKGs
SHORTY WAS HERE

HOW THE ANGEL GOT ON TOP OF THE CHRISTMAS TREE

This fairy tale answers that age old question, "How did the angel git on top of the Christmas tree?"

Santy wuz settin' there in front of the fireplace, laid out in the Lazy Boy with his feet up. Suddenly he woke up and glanced at his watch. It was 'leven thirty! It wuz Christmas Eve and he had to be outta there by twelve or he wouldn't git all the toys delivered in time!

He jumped up and run to the back room. He tore through the closet lookin' fer his red suit. He shook the moth balls outta the sleeve and slipped into the britches. He heard a great-big-RIP! He backed up to the mirro an' he'd tore the seat right outta them britches. He glanced at his watch and it wuz 25 'til twelve. So he skinned off the britches and run 'em down to the little tailor elves and said, "Boys, sew this back up!" And they did.

Santy come in and throwed on his coat 'n hunted 'round in the closet fer his boots. He couldn't find 'em 'n hollered, "Maw! Where's my boots at?" She said, "They're out on the back porch where you left 'em when ya come in last Christmas!" An' shurnuf, he run out on the back porch they'd built on the trailer house 'n there they were. He'd pulled 'em off wet last year and they'd dried out and curled up. He stuffed his feet down in 'em an' dadgum, if the heel didn't fall off the left boot! Santy glanced at his watch. It was 20 'til twelve! He ripped them boots off and took 'em down to the little cobbler elves and said, "Boys, hammer this back on!" And they did.

Santy slipped on his boots and run into the house, grabbed his coat and took out across the yard to hook up the sleigh. The yard light had burnt out and somebody'd left the fresno parked in the driveway. He hit that sucker at a high lope an' went head over heels and lit with a great big war whoop, spooked the reindeer an' they went over the top rail out into the beet tops! Santy glanced at his watch an' it wuz a quarter 'til twelve!

The little cowboy elves saddled up and brought the reindeer into the barn, put 'em in the hitch and hooked 'em up to the sleigh. Santy jumped up in the buckboard seat, cracked the whip 'n the reindeer took off, an' Santy jis sat there! The tugs had broke on the harness! Santy glanced at his watch. It wuz 10 'til twelve!

Santy said. "Boys, gather up them reindeer and I'll fix the harness." Then he hooked the team back up, leaped in the sleigh and slid on down in front of the house. Just as they pulled up to the house one of the runners fell off the sled! Santy glanced at his watch! It wuz 5 'til twelve!

They welded the runner back on and Santy run in the house. He grabbed that big bag o' toys, slung 'em over his shoulder . . . Yup, you guessed it. The bottom tore outta that bag and toys went everywhere!

Santy wuz down on his hands and knees, scrabblin' around stuffin' them toys in a Safeway bag when a little angel come flyin' in the door with a Christmas tree over his shoulder.

He said, "Santy, where you want me to put this?"

SANTA
CLAU
1990

THE SERMON ON THE CAN

Gather 'round me sinners
And I will go ahead
On a subject so disgusting
That angels fear to tread!

Some say it's an addiction
Some say it's a disease.
I've seen it take a healthy man
and bring him to his knees.

Though you try to hide it
There's little you can do.
'Cause tell tale signs begin to show up
In your attitude

The left side of your pickup
Turns a muddy brown
And little spots dog yer tracks
As you wander through the town

Yer lip begins to shrivel
And yer breath's like gasoline.
You start to wear a nice round hole
In the pocket of yer jeans.

Soon yer family shuns you
And friends give you the slip.
Little stains creep across
The corner of yer lip.

Heaven help the person
That's standin' in yer way,
When you run out an' have to go
Cold turkey for a day!

I beg you stop! Stop and look around!
And see what you've become!
An' it all began with a little pinch
Between yer cheek and gum.

I've told it like I see it
And I swear to you it's true.
I thank you for your time tonight.
Wonder if I could bum a chew?

SPLAT
PTT

CAMP COOKIE

He's the tumbleweed chef and rides with the wagon
Ahead of the thunderin' herd.
His pots and pans clack like a diamondback's rattle.
He growls or he don't say a word.

His face is a roadmap. Looks like a carcass
Hung too many days in the sun.
He smells like a mule and cooks with a shovel
And his fly is always undone.

The riders kin tell when he's in the kitchen,
The buzzards all come into view.
He spits in the pan and shaves in the taters
And clips his toenails in the stew.

His gunpowder biscuits explode in the fire.
His beans explode in yer bowel.
His medda lark souffle is hard on the belly,
They say it tastes 'bout like a owl.

His coffee's so rank a housefly won't touch it.
Even buckshot floats in the slop.
You don't pour a cup, you twist off a swaller,
Then chew a sip offa the top.

Now, cowboys are tough guys who face death each day
In blizzards or stampedes or storms.
They ride them bad horses and sleep with the snakes
And duel with the hooves and the horns.

But many a cowboy who follered the wagon
Has joined the 'last roundup club',
Not from Indians, gunfights or even bad whiskey
But from eatin' Camp Cookie's grub.

BOB BLACK

ALL NATURAL BEEF

It's true that my steer is all natural
I've dispensed with all vaccines and drugs
Not one pesticide is poured on his hide
He'd be lonesome without all his bugs!

The lice are his own peanut gallery
The ticks and the heel flies, too.
He scratches all day while they nibble away
But it does give him something to do.

I've no use for antibiotics.
For those drenches and potions and pills.
He's had a rough time, but now doin' fine,
Though he's pore as an ol' whippoorwill.

He's had ricketts and double pneumonia.
He's a veteran of all that I've learned.
Coccidiosis, Leptospirosis,
And the scours are waiting their turn.

So you see all you slavers of science
Who depend on hi tech for it all,
My steer is alive, weighs three twenty-five,
But, he only turned seven last fall!

ALL NATURAL BEEF RANCH
007
© 86

COWBOY PRESERVES

I've been searching for a reason as to why we live so long
Our life expectancy is hard to beat.
Some say it's easy livin' or medical research
But I think it's the preservatives I eat.

> Preservatives are everywhere. You might just be surprised.
> In Mayonnaise and Roman Meal bread.
> Smoked salmon, pickled herring, even some Granola bars.
> In margarine, the hard stick or the spread.

In diet pop and soy sauce and Kellogg's Special K,
The Aunt Jemima syrup that you bought.
In hot dogs and baloney and Betty Crocker Cake mix
And Tang, the choice of every astronaut.

> Oh, I eat roast beef and veggies, but I never overdo.
> Man cannot live by benzoates alone.
> Yet I crave the magic tingle that I get from my Parkay
> Or a Twinkie as it soaks into my bones.

My body now depends on the preservatives I eat.
I'm sure they retard spoilage of my brains.
I'll look forever youthful even through my twilight years
Because of their protection in my veins.

> Someday I'll just be sittin' in my rocker on the porch
> And everyone will say I'm lookin' great.
> Because I'll be so well preserved, no one will know I'm dead
> Unless they read my expiration date!

NUTRA
SULF
100% PURE
SULFUR
LOW IN CALO
HIGH IN FLAV
MOTHER'S
all Natural
GLOP
YIPPEE!!
MARVELOUS ON CEREAL!
ZESTY ON BURGERS!
PAINTS OVER NAILS! WON'T CHIP!
GREAT FOR LINOLEUM!
HOORAY!!
ROBLES JUNCTION, ARI
BIMBO'S
BIMBO'S ARTIFICAL COW JUICE
TO OPEN SINK TEETH IN BOX
%U.S.RDA %
VIT C...0
VIT B...0
VIT A...0
IRON...0
CALCIUM..0
ZINC...0
COPPER.0
GOLD...0
THIAMINE..0
NIACIN..0
FAT...0
SALT.30,000
PINE-TAR..89,000,000
Pest
NEW
Pest
Puggets.
TASTY LITTLE CHUNKS OF DRY-ROASTED PINE TAR IN A DELICIOUS COATING OF PURE ROCK SALT
SHEEP DIP OFFER
DETAILS ON BACK
WITH! WHITEWASH! SODIUM METABISULFITE! BHA! BHT! TBHQ! PROPYL GALLATE! and MSG!!!
BOB BLACK

LOONEY LUCY'S SPA AND HEALTH FOOD CO-OP

Come to Loony Lucy's spa and health food co-op
We serve the only fern kabob in town
If your spirit is depressed and your body needs a rest
We guarantee to turn your life around.

Your double chin will soon be doing chin ups
When you taste our own bermuda grass surprise
Your diet will consist of rose hips, knees and wrists
And soup concocted from potato eyes.

Remember T-Bone steaks with all the trimmings
And spareribs smoking in the open air
In Lucy's cooking class they're visions in your past.
Do your prefer your oatmeal done or rare?

Our imitation, atomized club sandwich
Is enriched with mold from thirty day old cheese
We feed you with a trowel and commune au natural
While soaking you in mayonnaise and peas.

We serve organic tea, unsweetened saccharine,
Crackers made from tadpole dingalings,
Decaffeinated beets and artificial meats
And season them with young grasshopper wings.

Forget your basic food nutrition courses
That stress a balanced diet like we learned
We'll fill you up with pills, give herbs to cure your ills,
And rub you down with scum from butter churns.

At Lucy's spa we have a rule to live by
That gives you help to eat the things you should
If you order dining out, whenever you're in doubt,
Just beware of any food that tastes good.

LOCATE OUR RESTROOMS BEFORE YOU EAT ~ BECAUSE YOU WON'T HAVE TIME TO ASK.
where nothing is real
Rubber Soup!
SQUEEZE ROOM
Today's Special THE PRAIRIE SUPRISE! just 4.95 HEARTY!!! APPETIZING!
WHAT YOU SEE ISN'T EVEN CLOSE TO WHAT YOU GET. Lucy

THE VEGETARIAN'S NIGHTMARE

a dissertation on plants' rights

Ladies and diners I make you
A shameful, degrading confession.
A deed of disgrace in the name of good taste
Though I did it, I meant no aggression.

I had planted a garden last April
And lovingly sang it a ballad.
But later in June beneath a full moon
Forgive me, I wanted a salad!

So I slipped out and fondled a carrot
Caressing its feathery top.
With the force of a brute I tore out the root!
It whimpered and came with a pop!

Then laying my hand on a radish
I jerked and it left a small crater.
Then with the blade of my True Value spade
I exhumed a slumbering tater!

Celery I plucked, I twisted a squash!
Tomatoes were wincing in fear.
I choked the Romaine. It screamed out in pain,
Their anguish was filling my ears!

I finally came to the lettuce
As it cringed at the top of the row
With one wicked slice I beheaded it twice
As it writhed, I dealt a death blow.

I butchered the onions and parsley.
My hoe was all covered with gore.
I chopped and I whacked without looking back
Then I stealthily slipped in the door.

My bounty lay naked and dying
So I drowned them to snuff out their life.
I sliced and I peeled as they thrashed and they reeled
On the cutting board under my knife.

I violated tomatoes
So their innards could never survive.
I grated and ground 'til they made not a sound
Then I boiled the tater alive!

Then I took the small broken pieces
I had tortured and killed with my hands
And tossed them together, heedless of whether
They suffered or made their demands.

I ate them. Forgive me, I'm sorry
But hear me, though I'm a beginner
Those plants feel pain, though it's hard to explain
To someone who eats them for dinner!

I intend to begin a crusade
For PLANT'S RIGHTS, including chick peas.
The A.C.L.U. will be helping me, too.
In the meantime, please pass the bleu cheese.

Doro Gill ©

DONATIN': RODEO STYLE

There's a piece of little finger on a fence out in Cheyenne
They had a wild horse race and I thought I'd lend a hand

I gave a bite of earlobe to a bronc in Calgary
A souvenir, I reckon, so he'd remember me

A hank of hair is clingin' to a light pole in Raton
Where we both went up together but I come down all alone

In Omaha, Nebraska I left a chunk of chin
I tried to find it later but I forgot where all I'd been

I left bone chips down in Tucson with a doctor and his nurse
Gave blood in Oklahoma just to help me reimburse

My pardners I was owin' for the gas to Angelo
Where I'd grudgingly donated a percentage of my toe

An Oakdale corriente took the tip off of my thumb
And this cast I got in Denver is a little cumbersome

A doggin' steer in Billings took a bit of this eyebrow
When he thought he'd do some farmin' and used me for a plow

A bull in Garden City took interest in my nose
And peeled the top off of it, for his scrapbook, I suppose

I've got shrapnel in my body from arenas far and near
From Bismarck, Cedar City, Winnemucca and Fort Pierre

Pendleton, Ellensburg, Shreveport and Dubuque
When I start to think about it, it makes me kinda spook

Though I've made quite a collection, I only think it's fair
'Cause pieces of my body I left scattered everywhere

Enough hide to make a riggin', enough hair to braid a rein
Enough teeth to make a necklace, enough nerve to build a brain

I've left a trail of things I've lost like heart and soul and mind
But them that went before me left some of theirs behind

So I borrowed'em and used'em like they meant for me to do
And I'll leave'em for the next guy and if that next guy's you

When you run short of courage or losin' gets you down
Remember them before you left somethin' in the ground

And in the chute or ropin' box or floatin' in the air
It's the ghost of every cowboy who ever entered there

Every ridin', ropin' outlaw left you some will to win
Just look around ya, pardner, you'll find a piece of skin.

FIVE FLAT

Now everyone I ever knew that did much work with stock
Has spent some time in practice throwin' houlihans at rocks
And be they real cowboys or pretenders with a hat
All dream of ropin' just one steer in five point nothin' flat

Now me, I'm not much differ'nt, I do a little dreamin'
And my dream is usually pleasant but I always wake up screamin'
It's a nightmare rank and scary and it turns me gravy pale
But since y'all are waitin' I'll continue with the tale.

I've made the National Finals way down in O. K. C.
And Leo Camarillo is my pardner, lucky me.
We're almost in the money when we get our final steer
And in my dream I always get to sweatin' right in here.

I'm backed up in the box as the whole crowd quiets down
I shoot a look at Leo and he nods, "Let's go to town!"
My horse is at the ready and the steer is pointed right
We need a 5 point 7 to be champions tonight.

I nod my head and out he comes, a'runnin' straight and true.
I hear the headgate clangin' and we're just a step or two
Behind the poundin' footsteps of that corriente ox.
I see my chance and throw it, not ten feet from the box.

Leo's like a vision of a 'willer' in the wind.
His smooth and graceful loop is flyin' under, down and in.
I look back past my shoulder, see him goin' to the horn
Then I feel that solid jerkin'; fer this moment I was born!

I spin around and face him; check the heels, he's got two!
I hear the flag a 'snappin' and the crowd has come unglued!
I glance up to the scoreboard as the speaker says, "FIVE FLAT!"
I can almost taste that buckle and I'm grinnin' like a cat.

But the crowd begins to groanin'. I get prickles on my skin.
The judge is flaggin' NO TIME and the panic's settin' in!
I look down at the critter, say a prayer but it's too late.
There my head loop, once so pretty, is now a figure eight!

Now Leo don't seem bothered, disappointment, he's above.
But, damn! I'm really hurtin' as I look down at my glove.
It's not humiliation or the fact that I look dumb
I usually wake up screamin' 'cause I've dallied up my thumb!

Don Gill
1982

ODE TO THE ANNOUNCER

Announcers are a special breed who constantly are looking
For better ways to please the crowd and keep the action cooking.

They've traded in their rhinestone suits they bought from Porter Wagoner
For fashion wear from Larry M and chaps stole from the flagger.

The cordless mike lets them work in places that seem silly
Do interviewing while they shake the dew off of their lily.

They're now announcing from a horse on mounts they beg or borrow
And often make the night's best ride to some bronc rider's sorrow.

I expect that we've just seen the beginning of their genius.
They'll be cowback at the Palace, and wetback at Salinas.

To offer better coverage, if no one minds the trouble,
They'll put two hand holds on the rig and ride the bareback double.

At places where the crowd is known as bad and needs a trouncing,
Then three or four will take the mike; they'll call it gang announcing.

As rodeos expand and grow they'll develop specialties.
Competing gays will need someone who's cute in B.V.D.'s

Prison rodeo announcers, for them that ropes and plunders,
Where both the rider and the bull will be called by the numbers.

Eventually nudist camps will rope down in the valley.
Announcers may be called upon to change what's called the dally.

So what's the future hold for them? Can so many make a living
Telling Dolly Parton jokes? Will wives go on forgiving?

Will clowns keep needing straight men for their monkeys, ducks and peacocks?
Will double nickels be repealed? Will they keep on making Maalox?

Will no one ever realize their job is fun and funny?
Will the unsuspecting public keep paying their good money?

I say, YES! And raise my glass. And drink down every ounce, sir!
To the master of the microphone . . . the RODEO ANNOUNCER!

COWBOY LOGIC

One morning bright and early we wuz goin' down the road.
The night before I'd missed my steer and Donny Boy got throwed.
But we wuz feelin' better when ol' Hard Luck bummed a ride.
He climbed up in the camper shell and settled down inside.

The pickup bed was fulla junk, our rodeoin' stuff.
But Hard Luck never said a word 'cause there was room enough.
The sun rose in our rear view on I-20, headed west.
And Hard Luck dozed then fell asleep. I guess he needed rest.

Then somewhere on the freeway we almost hit a bus.
I hit the brakes and skidded nearly killin' all of us.
Ol' Hard Luck's head bounced off the back, it sounded like a shot!
Like someone threw a bowling ball against a cast iron pot.

"You reckon we should check'im, Don?" "Nope," was all he said.
"He hit that sucker awful hard, I think he might be dead."
A look came in his beady eyes, like I had hay fer brains.
His logic was pure cowboy. While I listened, he explained:

"There ain't no point in stoppin' now. No reason on this earth.
If he's alive, he'll be okay until we reach Ft. Worth
And if he's dead as Coley's goat, he'll sure be hard to lift.
He'll be a damn site easier to move when he gits stiff!"

Leon's CAMPER CITY
FORT LUPTON
JACKALOPE CHARTER
BOB BLACK

LEGACY OF THE RODEO MAN

There's a hundred years of history and a hundred before that
All gathered in the thinkin' goin' on beneath his hat.
And back behind his eyeballs and pumpin' through his veins
Is the ghost of every cowboy that ever held the reins.

Every coil in his lasso's been thrown a million times
His quiet concentration's been distilled through ancient minds.
It's evolution workin' when the silver scratches hide
And a ghostly cowboy chorus fills his head and says, "Let's ride."

The famous and the rowdy, the savage and the sane
The bluebloods and the hotbloods and the corriente strain
All knew his mother's mothers or was his daddy's kin
'Til he's nearly purely cowboy, born to ride and bred to win.

He's got Buffalo Bill Cody and Goodnight's jigger boss
And all the brave blue soldiers that General Custer lost
The ghost of Pancho Villa, Sittin' Bull and Jessie James
All gathered by his campfire keepin' score and takin' names.

There's every Royal Mountie that ever got his man
And every day-work cowboy that ever made a hand
Each man that's rode before him, yup, every mother's son
Is in his corner, rootin', when he nods to make his run.

Freckles Brown might pull his bull rope, Casey Tibbs might jerk the flank,
Bill Pickett might be hazin' when he starts to turn the crank.
Plus Remington and Russell lookin' down his buckhorn sight
All watchin' through the window of this cowboy's eyes tonight.

And standin' in the catch pen or in chute number nine
Is the offspring of a mountain that's come down from olden time
A volcano waitin' quiet, 'til they climb upon his back
Rumblin' like the engine of a freight train on the track.

A cross between a she bear and a bad four wheel drive
With the fury of an eagle when it makes a power dive
A snake who's lost its caution or a badger gone berserk
He's a screamin', stompin', clawin', rabid, mad dog piece o' work.

From the rollers in his nostrils to the foam upon his lips
From the hooves as hard as granite to the horns with dagger tips
From the flat black starin' shark's eye that's the mirror of his soul
Shines the challenge to each cowboy like the devil callin' roll.

In the seconds that tick slowly 'til he climbs upon his back
Each rider faces down the fear that makes his mouth go slack
And cuts his guts to ribbons and gives his tongue a coat
He swallows back the panic gorge that's risin' in his throat.

The smell of hot blue copper fills the air around his head
Then a single, solid, shiver shakes away the doubt and dread
The cold flame burns within him 'til his skin's as cold as ice
And the dues he paid to get here are worth every sacrifice

All the miles spent sleepy drivin', all the money down the drain
All the "if I's" and the "nearly's," all the bandages and pain
All the female tears left dryin', all the fever and the fight
Are just a small downpayment on the ride he makes tonight.

And his pardner in this madness that the cowboy's call a game
Is a ton of buckin' thunder bent on provin' why he came
But the cowboy never wavers he intends to do his best
And of that widow maker he expects of him no less.

There's a solemn silent moment that every rider knows
When time stops on a heartbeat like the earth itself was froze
Then all the ancient instinct fills the space between his ears
'Til the whispers of his phantoms are the only thing he hears

When you get down to the cuttin' and the leather touches hide
And there's nothin' left to think about, he nods and says, "Outside!"
Then frozen for an instant against the open gate
Is hist'ry turned to flesh and blood, a warrior incarnate.

And while they pose like statues in that flicker of an eye
There's somethin' almost sacred, you can see it if you try.
It's guts and love and glory — one mortal's chance at fame
His legacy is rodeo and cowboy is his name.

"Turn 'im out"

photo by SUE ROSOFF

About the Artists . . .

DON GILL – An Idaho raised cowboy in traditional buckaroo country. He and his family live on their small ranch near King Hill. He has illustrated Baxter's first five books as well as many others. His calendars and prints continue to capture the everyday cowboy calamities that are a part of ranch living.

Buckaroo purists and workin' cowboys will note that Don's cowdogs, critters, coyotes, cayuses and cowboys all have the faint aroma of familiarity.

Artists will note, with respect, that it's not easy to make a dog look demented, a cow look evil or a horse look disgusted. Don can do it. He is a cowboy artist of the finest kind.

BOB BLACK – The only baby ever actually to be dropped on his head by the stork. His father was heard to remark, "it's bad luck for that boy if the flattop ever goes outta style."

Overcoming his deformity by wearing merely the brim of a hat, Bob soon gained popularity billing himself as "The Great Punzo! Dog Trainer to the Stars!" It was here that his artist's blood began to surge. He took to scrimshawing the teeth of his charges. Pooches all over town suddenly had dentition bearing miniature engravings of tap dancing bovines or horses eluding dull political speeches and the like.

Then, while vacationing at a truck stop just this side of Fort Lupton, Colorado, inspiration bonked him on the noggin! He crawled under the nearest eighteen-wheeler (an emergency shipment of lard on it's way to Nogales) and using the reflective chrome on one of the mudflaps, illustrated his brother's poems!

The artist lives in a hollow tree somewhere on the West Coast and breaks hornets for a living.

More About the Artists . . .

JAY ADAMS – Father of 2 — Husband of 1 — residing in the one-horse town of Alamosa, Colorado. Slaving over the counter as manager/salesman of an Auto & Truck parts store during the day, while fulfilling his dream of becoming a full-fledged artist in the wee hours of the night.

JAN SWAN GIFFORD – Married to an unsuspecting cowboy, lives on a ranch near Buffalo, South Dakota in tropical Harding County. Draws, paints, admires good horses, and raises registered barn cats for profit.

CHERYL HAWES – Lives with banker-roper husband and 2 children on a small Oregon sheep ranch where she creates and sells greeting cards in an attempt to justify her chronic letter writing tendencies.

CHARLES MARSH – Lives in Center City, Philadelphia and draws humorous illustrations including *"Cow Country"* and *"Pig Tales"* which appear monthly in Farm Journal publications.

THERESA SCHLEIGH – Ranch raised, married and cowboy's for a living in Oregon and California. In addition to cartooning on her TS Cattle Company ranch, she does western oils and bronzes.

ACE REID – Ace is the dean of cowboy cartoonists. He and Madge live in Texas where he produces *Cowpokes,* one of America's most widely syndicated cowboy cartoons.

SUE ROSOFF – Photographer, currently residing in Berkeley, who began documenting the sport and culture of professional rodeo as a master's thesis at University of California in Berkeley in 1981 and is now addicted.

About the Author . . .

Baxter grew up in New Mexico. He received his Doctor of Veterinary Medicine degree in 1969. He practiced in feedlots and on ranches in the mountain west. Since 1983 he has been a full-time cowboy poet entertaining at banquets, fairs, goat ropin's and cow camps.

Baxter's weekly column, *On the Edge of Common Sense,* is the most widely syndicated agriculture column in America. He describes it as mostly humorous, occasionally political and accidentally informative.

He lives in Colorado with his wife Cindylou and his daughter Jenny.

The End